The dragon is an age-old symbol of the highest spiritual essence, embodying wisdom, strength, and the divine power of transformation. In this spirit, Shambhala Dragon Editions offers a treasury of readings in the sacred knowledge of Asia. In presenting the works of authors both ancient and modern, we seek to make these teachings accessible to lovers of wisdom everywhere.

THE AWAKENED ONE

A Life of the Buddha

Sherab Chödzin Kohn

SHAMBHALA

Boston

2000

For my mother,
Leona Kohn,
on her eightieth birthday

Shambhala Publications, Inc.
Horticultural Hall
300 Massachusetts Avenue
Boston, Massachusetts 02115
www.shambhala.com

Printed in the United States of America
⊗*This edition is printed on acid-free paper that meets the*
American National Standards Institute Z39.48 Standard

Distributed in the United States by Random House, Inc., and
in Canada by Random House of Canada Ltd

Library of Congress Cataloging-in-Publication Data

Chödzin, Sherab.
The awakened one: a life of the Buddha / Sherab Chödzin Kohn.
p.   cm. — (Shambhala dragon editions)
ISBN 1–57062–551–4
1. Gautama Buddha.   I. Title.
BQ882.C47   1994
294.3'63 — dc20   93-26122
[B]   CIP
BVG 01

Contents

Dharma but decides not to teach • The god Sahampati
• Trapusha and Bhallika take refuge • Upaka on the road
• The Four Noble Truths and the Eightfold Path
• The first five arhats • The doctrine of nonself
• The conversion of Yasha and his friends • The Buddha
disperses the Sangha • The pleasure outing • The three
Kashyapas

Acknowledgments

A GREAT NUMBER OF WORKS have been consulted in the preparation of this book. I confine myself here to indicating those which I drew upon significantly. Primary were three traditional sources: the Pali canon, the *Lalitavishtara Sutra*, and the *Buddhacharita* by Ashvagosha. As to the Pali canon, I owe much to the invaluable selection, arrangement, and retranslation of texts from that vast treasure store of scripture made by the distinguished English Theravada monk Bhikku Nyanamoli. These are presented in his *Life of the Buddha* (Kandy, Ceylon: Buddhist Publication Society, 1972). The *Lalitavishtara Sutra* is a Sanskrit work of Sarvastivada/Mahayana cast, dating roughly from the beginning of the first millennium CE. It is found most reliably in English as *The Voice of the Buddha*, 2 vols, trans. by Gwendolyn Bays (Berkeley: Dharma Publishing, 1983). E. H. Johnston's is the best and only complete English translation of the Ashvaghosha; it is based on both Sanskrit and Tibetan source material. Johnston's rendering of this great verse life of the Buddha, which also dates from the early part of the first millennium, appears in two separate parts. The first part is Asvaghosa's *Buddhacarita* (Lahore, India: Motilal Banarsidass, 1936). The second part appeared serially in the journal *Acta Orientalia*. In passages quoted from material using Pali terms, Sanskrit equivalents have been substituted for the sake of reader continuity.

Also material were W. Woodville Rockhill (trans.), *Life of the Buddha* (Varanasi, India: Orientalia Indica, 1884; reprint 1972), which translates excerpts from Tibetan canonical works; T. W. Rhys Davids's classic translation, *Buddhist Birth Stories* (London: Trübner & Co., 1880); P. Bigandet (trans.), *The Life or Legend of Gaudama: The Buddha of the Burmese*, 2 vols. (Varanasi, India: Bharatiya Publishing House, 1879; reprint 1979); and Narada Maha Thera, *The Buddha and His Teachings* (Kandy, Sri Lanka: Buddhist Publication Society, 1979). Mention should also be made of Ananda K. Coomaraswamy, *Buddha and the Gospel of Buddhism* (New Delhi: Munshiram Manoharlat Publishers, 1974), and Etienne Lamotte's monumental *Histoire du bouddhisme indien* (Université de Louvain, 1958; reprint 1976), where precise and comprehensive references can always be found. Also helpful was E. J. Thomas, *The Life of the Buddha* (London: Routledge & Kegan Paul Ltd, 1969).

Introduction

THE STORY OF A HUMAN LIFE grips us very directly because it is a case history of the condition we all share. Since beginningless time people have listened to stories of what others have done, feeling for the pattern in life these stories might reveal, exploring for their own possibilities, their own boundaries. We want to know where life can go, what can be made of it, how far its scope can extend. Are there barriers? Are there hidden treasures? Though we may appear settled, we are always testing, testing at our edges and limits or retreating from having done so. Convention, ordinary life, provides an artificial definition and an artificial safe haven. But the walls of convention are thin. If we pass through them, what is the real reach and range of existence that lies beyond?

In the context of this basic questioning, the life of the Buddha is an immense landmark. The Buddha was a prince, and he left the palace. He stepped out of the pattern that he had grown into and set out on a journey of discovery from which he never returned. He might have been discouraged and beaten and fallen back on the easy life, or he might have followed a sidetrack into insanity. But instead he completed his journey. The Buddha fully explored the true reach and range of reality. He set out to conquer death, and he actually did so. This is what makes him a hero for us, an exemplar. That is why his life story is particularly gripping.

First he discovered that there is no safety. The basic weather of existence — impermanence — beats mercilessly upon whatever we try to erect against it. No stuff of dreams, no cocoon of convention, can withstand change, aging, and death. So the prince reluctantly renounced clinging to the illusion of security and sought the reality beyond it. Relentlessly, with unflagging courage and devotion, he followed the path pointed out by intelligence. The result? A prince completely awoke from all dreams and became a buddha, an awakened one.

A mantra enshrined in *The Heart Sutra*, a key Buddhist text, runs, *Gate gate paragate parasamgate bodhi svaha*. "Gone, gone, gone beyond, gone completely beyond, awake, so be it." That limns the first part of the Buddha's story.

The rest of the story is the down-to-earth pageantry of wisdom and compassion. The "Thus-Gone One," the Tathagata, as the Buddha is called, clearly sees the totality of existence and beyond existence. He sees the parameters of all that is and how they are constituted, how the whole thing works and does not really work. Does he come back to those he left behind who are still earnestly slumbering, passionately caught up in dreams, and find a way to open and clear their eyes? At first, knowing the difficulty, the Tathagata decides to remain silent (a tendency he constantly reverted to ever after). But waking and sleeping—the Buddha and confused beings—are inseparably bound together, part of the same magic. This truth is acted out in our story by a god who appears and entreats the Buddha to teach. He arouses the Tathagata's fathomless compassion, and from there unfold forty-five years of communicating, of teaching the Dharma. The Dharma is the wisdom of total vision, which can be boiled down to knowing in specific circumstances what should be cultivated and what should be refrained from. The Buddha's forty-five years of teaching required a mountainous labor of patience and care, not to mention an incalculable amount of walking. And it did an incalculable amount of good, as we shall see.

There exists a large and complex body of material on the Buddha's life. It is preserved in writing in ancient texts of various Buddhist traditions and in various languages. It lives orally on the tongues of

Buddhist teachers of a great variety of national and sectarian persuasions, who continue to use the Buddha's life as an example. Perhaps the most vital and forceful point is that the Buddha continues to be emulated widely. Of course there are many Buddhists trying to follow the main part of his example — to meditate with discipline and knowledge and so attain enlightenment. But the Buddha's story continues to live also in many small, earthy ways, as when a rising teacher looks out among his students to see who are to be his two leading disciples, his Shariputra and Maudgalyayana; or when the long-time personal attendant of an aged and preeminent Tibetan guru massages his teacher's tired old limbs, both knowing well that Ananda did this for the Buddha.

And of course there is not only the material direct out of the Buddha's own tradition. In addition, the great teacher's life has been variously purveyed and worked over by scholars and other writers with a non-Buddhist optic, here and there with considerable merit.

In telling the Buddha's story I have tried to follow what seemed to me a straightforward path. I saw the tradition as a living whole and did not approach it with any set of conceptual instruments such as one might use to try to cut away legend from history or to sever the tissue of one tradition from that of another. Rather my approach has been that of a composer who, awestruck by the dignity and beauty of an ancient and manifold song cycle, preserves its essence, integrity, and inalienable features in a unified chamber piece of manageable length. I hope I may have succeeded to some degree.

My heartfelt thanks to my guru, the Vidyadhara Trungpa Rinpoche, without whom I would be deaf, dumb, and blind; to my publisher Samuel Bercholz, who requested this work; and to my wife, Judith Kohn, who plays cheerfully as we tumble together through space.

THE
AWAKENED
ONE

1

Birth, Youth, Renunciation

SHAKYAMUNI BUDDHA, THE AWAKENED ONE, recounted his own story to his close disciple Ananda.

Through countless lives, he was a bodhisattva, one who is on the path of awakening, who labored and sacrificed for the benefit of other beings. In a past age of the world, as a forest-dwelling ascetic named Sumedha, he threw himself at the feet of an earlier buddha, Dipankara, and resolved to become a buddha himself. Dipankara looked down and saw the bodhisattva lying in the mud before him, offering his body as a plank to be walked upon so that the Buddha would not have to soil his feet. He paused in his progress and prophesied to the multitude that accompanied him everywhere that after many eons this young ascetic would indeed also become a buddha. Through many subsequent lives, the bodhisattva practiced the ten transcendental virtues that prepare the way to buddhahood, complete enlightenment. Finally, when he had neared perfection of compassion and understanding, he took birth as a god in the fourth heaven of the desire realm, Tushita, the Heaven of the Contented. There, as Bearer of the White Banner, Shvetaketu, he shone as the teacher and king of a hundred thousand long-lived gods. That life in the Heaven of the Contented had already gone on for many thousands of years when the bodhisattva heard a tumultuous sound resounding through the entire universe, the uproar caused by all the gods of the three thousand world systems telling each other that at last the time had come for the bodhisattva to attain buddhahood. On three kinds of occasions is such an uproar heard: when a world age is to end in destruction, when a universal monarch is to be born, and when a buddha is to be born. Now all the gods gathered in the Heaven of the Contented and implored Bearer of the White Banner not to let the moment pass, but to be born on earth and become a buddha for the sake of all sentient beings.

The future buddha deliberated. Was this the right time for a buddha to be born? As a world age progresses, the life span of human beings continually decreases. If a Buddha appears at a time when the human life span is a hundred thousand years, then old age, sickness, and dying, the alarm signals of impermanence, do not make a strong enough impression on people. There is little interest in the Dharma, the Teaching of the Buddha that conquers death. On the other hand, when the time has come when people live only twenty or thirty years, their few years are thronged with aggression and desire and clouded by depression. They are not uplifted enough to aspire to the Dharma, nor do they have time to practice it. Thus, when people live too long, they become intoxicated by eternity. When their life is too brief, they are crushed down by nihilism. A life span of about one hundred years is deemed ideal for the appearance of a Buddha.

As the life span of people on earth was not too far off the mark, the bodhisattva adjudged that his time had come. Then he deliberated further over the circumstances of his birth. On what continent, in what country, into what lineage, and to what mother should he be born?

When he had decided these things, the bodhisattva convoked an assembly of the gods of the Heaven of the Contented and taught the Dharma there for the last time. Then he announced his departure. Those Tushita gods were full of grief. They tried to persuade the bodhisattva to stay his decision. If he were to leave them, they pleaded, they would be bereaved of their teacher. There would be no luminary to guide and inspire them in their incalculably long existence. Without him, their realm and life would lose its luster. In response, Bearer of the White Banner took the crown from his head and placed it on the head of the bodhisattva Maitreya, who was also an inhabitant of Tushita and was already destined to be the buddha of the future age. "Lord Maitreya will teach you the Dharma when I am gone," he proclaimed. And to Maitreya he said, "You, Wise One, will be the first after me to attain supreme and perfect enlightenment." Then he went to the Nandana Grove in the capital of the Heaven of the Contented, and there, mindfully and fully aware, he died. At the same moment, fully mindful and aware, he entered his earthly mother's womb.

Also at that moment, a boundless light appeared throughout the worlds. Even in the dark abysses of space where neither sun nor moon shines, this light shone, and the beings living in those places saw each other for the first time, and said, "It seems that other creatures have been born here!" Throughout all the world systems, the fundamental solid earth element trembled and shook.

IT WAS IN the middle of the first millennium BCE that the bodhisattva took his final birth, on Jambudvipa, the southern continent of this world system, in the country of the Shakyas, which lay in the foothills of the Himalayas in present-day southern Nepal. His father, Shuddhodana, was the king of the Shakyas. As befitted a king, he was of the kshatriya, or warrior, caste, and his clan lineage, that of the Gautamas, was ancient and pure. The bodhisattva's mother was Mahamaya, the daughter of Suprabuddha, a powerful Shakyan noble. Since the bodhisattva was born a prince of the Shakyas, after his enlightenment he was known as the sage of the Shakyas, Shakyamuni. Since his clan name was Gautama, he was later also called Gautama Buddha.

One night during the midsummer festival in Kapilavastu, Queen Mahamaya had a dream. In the dream she ascended a height, and a large and beautiful white elephant with six tusks entered her womb through her right side. Then a great multitude bowed down to her.

When she awoke, she had a feeling of great well-being and knew she was with child. Indeed, she thought she could already see the child completely and perfectly formed within her womb, as one sees the colored thread running through a clear bead.

When she told the king of this, he called his brahmin wise men, who were versed in astrology and the interpretation of dreams. The brahmins told the king that a son would be born to him who would have the thirty-two major marks and the eighty minor marks of a great being. If he remained in the palace and pursued a worldly life, he would become a chakravartin, a universal monarch. However, if he renounced his home, wealth, and position and wandered forth as a holy man, he would become a completely enlightened buddha, and satisfy all beings with the elixir of deathlessness. The king was very pleased with these predictions. He gave the brahmins rich gifts and distributed food and gifts to the people.

During the time the queen was bearing the bodhisattva, she was without pain or sickness. In fact, she was radiant with unusually good health and was able to impart health to others. Many were the sick or mentally troubled ones whom she healed during this time by her mere touch or by means of her herbal preparations. The king for the most part put aside the business of state and devoted himself principally to religious rites, austerities, and acts of charity. It was a prosperous and happy time in the city. The weather was good. Trouble and conflict faded from people's lives.

Mahamaya's pregnancy lasted ten months. It was springtime, in the month of Vaishakha, when she began to feel the imminence of the birth. She asked to be taken to Lumbini, a pleasure grove belonging to her family that she had loved as a girl. Shuddhodana gave orders, and a great train of nobles, courtiers, and servants issued from the city to accompany her there. Colorful tents housing comfortable living quarters were set up, and all preparations were made for the birth. In the middle of the month, on the full-moon day, Queen Mahamaya was walking in the grove when suddenly she felt heavy and raised her right arm to take hold of a tree branch for support. Just then, as she stood grasping the branch, the bodhisattva was born into the world, instantly and painlessly. Once again a light shone through the worlds and the earth shook. Then the bodhisattva, who already had the form of a small child, took seven firm steps, looked into the four directions, and said, "I am the leader of the world, the guide of the world. This is my final birth." Two spouts of water, one warm and one cool, issued from the air above the bodhisattva's head and poured their pure and soothing waters over him. Thus washed, he was placed on a couch covered with silk brocades, and a white parasol was raised above his head.

At that time, a great rishi, a seer, named Asita was living alone in the mountains practicing meditation. He saw with his clear sight that a momentous and auspicious birth had taken place somewhere in the world. He performed divination and determined that this event had occurred at the court of King Shuddhodana, lord of the Shakyas. With his sister's son Naradatta he traveled to Kapilavastu. Being a renowned rishi, he was admitted at once to the court, and the king received him with deference, offering him water to wash his feet. When the formalities were at an end, the seer explained that he had seen visions of an auspicious birth, which he believed to be that of the king's son. He asked to see the child. Shuddhodana commanded his son to be brought. On seeing the child, the seer, despite his age and venerable status, rose from his seat and prostrated to the child, then placed the bodhisattva's feet on his head. Shuddhodana, stunned and impressed by this act of veneration on the part of the great rishi, also prostrated to his son. Then Asita examined the child and found on his body all the thirty-two major and eighty minor marks of a great being. He said that for a possessor of these marks, only two destinies were possible. Such a great being would become a universal monarch should he pursue a worldly life, or a completely enlightened buddha should he renounce worldly life and enter a life of homelessness devoted to spiritual truth.

Asita proclaimed this good news to the king. But after a short time, when his first joy had subsided, the old man unaccountably began to weep. Shuddodana's heart was touched with darkness. Could the good fortune that had come upon him hold a secret flaw? Had Asita seen some misfortune lying in his son's future? Anxiously he questioned the old seer. Asita, grasping the king's fears, was quick to reassure him. No misfortune lay ahead. He had experienced first joy and then grief, he explained, because first he had seen the greatness of the child. Then in a flash he had beheld his incomparable destiny. The child would surely renounce family, wealth, and position to seek spiritual truth. He would fully conquer delusion and become a buddha, a fully awakened one, such a one as appeared once in oceans of millennia. He would teach a doctrine that would free beings from the suffering of birth, old age, sickness, and death. And then Asita had experienced unspeakable grief, for he had realized that he, an old man, would not live to benefit from this buddha's teaching.

"Though I have mastered the four levels of meditative absorption," he explained to the king, "I have not been fully liberated from grasping and fixation. I have not drunk the pure elixir of deathlessness. And since I will not live to hear the Buddha teach, I will die without attaining the ultimate realization."

Shortly, Asita regained his composure and took his leave of the king. After leaving the palace, he spoke to his nephew Naradatta. "Start now to prepare yourself for the Buddha's teaching. Renounce the worldly life and meditate in solitude. Yet keep well informed of King Shuddhodana's son. When you hear that he has attained buddhahood, go to him and receive his teaching." More than thirty-five years later, after the Buddha had attained enlightenment, Naradatta would become his disciple, and not long after, meditating again in solitude, attain the fourth stage of realization, that of an arhat.

On the fifth day after the bodhisattva's birth, Shuddhodana called for the traditional naming ceremony to be performed. Nobles, courtiers, and brahmins were invited in large numbers. Food and drink was plentiful, and generous gifts were made to all. The boy was given the name Siddhartha, which means "accomplishment of the goal." Then eight skilled brahmins were asked to examine him and to augur his future. The eight brahmins all found the major and the minor marks, and seven of the eight predicted what the brahmins had predicted before. If he pursued the householder's life, he would become a universal monarch. If he renounced it and entered homelessness, he would become a fully enlightened buddha. But one of the eight, a young man named Kaundinya, clearly foresaw a single destiny for the boy — that of a buddha — and so proclaimed to the king. Years later, Kaundinya would become the first to attain realization through the Buddha's teaching.

Seven days after the Buddha's birth, Queen Mahamaya died. Her sister Mahaprajapati Gautami, who was also married to King Shuddhodana, was chosen to nurse and raise the child. Mahaprajapati was full of love for her sister's son and raised him like her own favorite.

For King Shuddhodana, all the wondrous events surrounding his son's arrival had been a source of gladness, but they had also been uncanny and had cast a shadow of awe and uncertainty. Queen Mahamaya's death again touched this darker side. In his moment of loss, his mind came to rest on the equivocal predictions of the brahmins. His son would be either a universal monarch or a buddha. True, greatness and glory lay with either, but it was now the former possibility that became enshrined in the king's heart. If his son succeeded him and became a great ruler, all the king's wishes would be fulfilled. But if the prince abandoned royal place and position, Shuddhodana would be without an heir — his house would be empty. This possibility now became a menace to be warded off. Thus he set about doing everything in his power to make matters take the desired turn. He carefully sheltered the prince from the world and surrounded him with luxury and pleasures. If the prince found nothing more to wish for, the king thought, the notion of abandoning the palace would never occur to him.

ONE DAY, WHEN the bodhisattva was still a small boy, a plowing festival took place. The king and queen (for Mahaprajapati now took her sister's

place), the nobles and servants, and much of the populace of Kapilavastu went out into the farming country beyond the city to a
specially prepared site. The king and other nobles were to inaugurate
the work of the season by plowing the first symbolic furrows. Gaily
caparisoned teams of oxen, yoked to plows brightly painted and
adorned with gold leaf, stood in readiness. Musicians played lively
music. People shouted and laughed. Children ran here and there.
Everyone was caught up in the excitement.

A couch was set up for Siddhartha in a sheltered area away from the
bustle of the crowd in the shade of a rose-apple tree. He was left in
the care of his nurses who were to take turns looking after him. As the
festival progressed, the nurses too were drawn into the festivities. First
one then another drifted away to watch the goings-on. After a considerable time, seeing one another, they suddenly realized that no one had
stayed to mind the prince. They rushed back and found the boy sitting,
composed and erect, in deep meditative absorption under the tree. To
their astonishment, though nearly two hours had elapsed and the sun
had changed its position, the shadow of the tree had remained station-
ary and continued to protect the bodhisattva from the intensity of the
sun's direct rays.

The news of this wonder was brought to King Shuddhodana, who
came in haste to see it with his own eyes. Seeing his son's radiant
composure, he prostrated to the bodhisattva, saying, "So, my dear son, I
bow to you for the second time."

As the boy grew older, the king redoubled his efforts to bind him to
the palace. He surrounded Siddhartha with scores of unblemished
beauties who were skilled in singing, dancing, and playing musical
instruments. Beautiful women, in constantly changing variety, accompanied the prince always, seeking in every way to divert and entertain
him and provide him with pleasure. Beautiful rooms with rich furnish-
ings and lushly planted roof gardens with gorgeous silken canopies
were the prince's daily haunts. Much of the time he did not even
descend to the lower stories of the palace.

The Buddha recalled his youth in these words: "I was delicate, most delicate, supremely delicate. Lily pools were made for me at my father's house solely for my benefit. Blue lilies flowered in one, white lilies in another, red lilies in a third. I used no sandalwood that was not from Varanasi. My turban, tunic, lower garments, and cloak were all made of Varanasi cloth. A white sunshade was held over me day and night so that no cold or heat or dust or grit or dew might inconvenience me.

"I had three palaces; one for the Winter, one for the Summer, and one for the Rains. In the Rains palace I was entertained by minstrels, all of them women. For the four months of the Rains I never went down to the lower palace. Though meals of broken rice with lentil soup are given to the servants and retainers in other people's houses, in my father's house, white rice and meat was given to them."[1]

When Siddhartha reached the age of sixteen, Shuddhodana decided that to forestall restlessness and draw him further into the householder's life, it would be good for the youth to marry. He had inquiries made among the noble families of Kapilavastu to see which among them might provide a suitable bride. In the business of arranging a marriage for Siddhartha, the king found that it was necessary to be able to proclaim the prince's accomplishments. A future king must be well educated and able to display prowess in the martial arts. But until this time, Siddhartha had done little beyond living a life of diversion and pleasure, shut away in one or another of his palaces.

Accordingly, much attention was now given to the prince's training, and it quickly became evident to everyone that he was exceedingly gifted in both intellectual and physical domains. He mastered all that could be taught him with astonishing speed. Contests among the sons of the city's gentry were arranged in which Siddhartha was to compete. In reading, writing, and mathematics, he not only far outshone all the sons of the Shakyan nobles, but even outstripped the teachers and erudite men of the kingdom. It was the same in the physical disciplines. In running, contests of strength, use of weaponry, and particularly in archery, he far surpassed all others. The nearly full-grown youth was strong and fleet of foot, and he was also well formed and beautiful to look at.

Not long after the competitions, a suitable bride was chosen for the prince. She was Yashodhara, a dignified and beautiful young woman, the daughter of a Shakyan noble family. A royal wedding was held, and the young woman came to share Siddhartha's life in the palace.

For the next dozen years little changed in the conditions of Siddhartha's life. King Shuddhodana, always in fear of the prophecies of the brahmins, continued to spare neither trouble nor expense in sheltering and pampering the prince. He continued to embellish the comforts of the palaces and gardens where the prince whiled away the three seasons and to surround him with beautiful women who captivated him with music and song and sexual pleasures.

The prince was bound not only by this carefree life of pleasure, but also by strong ties of family and position. Nonetheless in the course of time the spell of the palace wore thin. When the sorrows and limitations of ordinary life finally began to beat in upon the prince, they struck him almost as an insult, an insolent intrusion. And they made an extremely strong impression on him.

The Buddha later recounted: "While I had such power and good fortune, yet I thought: When an untaught ordinary man, who is subject to aging, not safe from aging, sees another who is aged, he is shocked, humiliated, and disgusted; for he forgets that he himself is no exception. But I too am subject to aging, not safe from aging, and so it cannot befit me to be shocked, humiliated, and disgusted on seeing another who is aged. When I considered this, the vanity of youth entirely left me.

"I thought: When an untaught ordinary man, who is subject to sickness, not safe from sickness, sees another who is sick, he is shocked, humiliated, and disgusted; for he forgets that he himself is no exception. But I too am subject to sickness, not safe from sickness, and so it cannot befit me to be shocked, humiliated, and disgusted on seeing another who is sick. When I considered this, the vanity of health entirely left me.

"I thought: When an untaught ordinary man, who is subject to death, not safe from death, sees another who is dead, he is shocked, humiliated, and disgusted, for he forgets that he himself is no exception. But I too am subject to death, not safe from death, and so it cannot befit me to be shocked, humiliated, and disgusted on seeing another who is dead. When I considered this, the vanity of life entirely left me."[2]

Tradition tells us of four encounters that finally shattered the bodhisattva's contentment with his life of pleasure.

The prince had a charioteer named Chandaka whom he used to have take him on occasional outings. These outings were well orchestrated by those whom Shuddhodana had placed in charge of the prince's service. Care was always taken to clear and decorate the way, and especially to remove anything ugly or unpleasant that might disturb the prince's mood.

One day, when the prince was already in his late twenties, he commanded Chandaka to take him to a particular garden to spend the afternoon. On the way, alongside the road they encountered a man bent over with age. His hair was gray and sparse, his face wizened. His eyes were red around the edges and had cataracts. His hands shook and his gait was unsteady as he walked feebly, leaning on a stick. The prince asked Chandaka, "Who is that man? The hairs of his head do not seem to resemble those of other people. His eyes also are strange, and he walks so oddly."

Chandaka replied, "Lord, that is an old man. He is that way because of the effect time has on everyone who is born. What that man has are the afflictions of old age that await all of us. The skin dries and wrinkles, the hair loses its color and falls out, the veins and arteries stiffen, the flesh loses its suppleness and shapelessly sags. We are beset with pains. Our eyes skin over and get red. The rest of our senses grow feeble. In fact, as time goes on, our whole body winds up with little strength left in it, hardly enough to move along, as you see with that old fellow there."

When the prince heard this explanation, he became frightened and upset. Instead of continuing on to the garden as he had intended, he ordered Chandaka to turn around and return to the palace.

King Shuddhodana saw the chariot returning and sent a messenger to inquire why his son had come back so early from his afternoon's diversion. When he heard the story, a cloud passed over his heart and he recalled the brahmins' prophecies. He ordered yet more elaborate entertainments to be arranged for the prince and an even greater number of beautiful women to be provided for his amusement. He also ordered a numerous guard to be mustered to keep watch on the palace.

Out driving in his chariot once again, by the side of the road Siddhartha saw a man suffering from disease. He was emaciated and pale. Parts of his body were swollen and other parts were covered with sores. He was leaning on another man for support and occasionally emitted piteous cries of pain. When Chandaka explained to Siddhartha what disease was, rather than continue with his outing, the prince returned to the palace deeply troubled.

When he heard the story of this incident, King Shuddhodana's concern deepened further, and he began to wonder what else he could do to fend off destiny. He felt that if only Siddhartha could be induced to remain at home for another short period of time, the crisis would pass and in the fullness of time, his son would become a great king.

On a third occasion driving in his chariot, the prince encountered a funeral procession. He saw a corpse being borne on a litter followed by bereaved relatives wailing, tearing their clothes, and covering themselves with ashes. He asked Chandaka to explain this horrifying spectacle.

"My prince, do you not know?" Chandaka answered. "This man lying on the litter is dead. His life has come to an end. His senses and feelings and consciousness have departed forever. He has become just like a log or a bundle of hay. Those relatives of his who have cared for him and cherished him through his life will never see him again. Without exception, everything that is born must die."

"But if everyone who has been born must come to this end," the prince replied, "how is it that everyone is not afraid? Their hearts must be very hard, for I see everyone going about their business as though nothing were the matter." In deep distress, the prince commanded Chandaka to return to the palace.

Hearing of this, Shuddhodana doubled the guard and told them to watch night and day to prevent the prince's departure.

On a fourth occasion when the bodhisattva was out driving in his chariot with Chandaka, he encountered a mendicant with upright bearing and a serene and radiant countenance. Siddhartha was impressed by this sight and questioned Chandaka about the man. Chandaka replied, "This is a holy man who has renounced worldly life and entered upon a life of homelessness. Such homeless mendicants devote themselves to spiritual pursuits such as meditation or practicing austerities. They have no possessions but wander from place to place, begging their daily food."

In deep thought, the prince had himself driven back to the palace.

To divert his son from his preoccupations, the king decided to send him on a visit to a nearby farming village. He hoped that Siddhartha would take an interest in the methods of the farmers. But when he got there, the delicate youth saw the toiling workers, dirty and half-clad, streaming with sweat as they struggled in the heat of the sun. The oxen were laden with heavy yokes that rubbed the hide from their shoulders. The plows they pulled bruised the earth and destroyed worms and insects in their progress. To force the beasts to work, the farmers had to prod them with iron goads that made their straining flanks run with blood. Slaver and foam dripped from their mouths as they were forced to drag the heavy plows over long distances. Thick clouds of gnats and stinging flies never ceased to torment them.

The prince was overcome with revulsion. When he learned that the laborers were his father's slaves, he freed them on the spot, telling them, "From today, you will no longer be slaves. You are free to go wherever you like and live in happiness." He also released the oxen, saying to them, "Go. From now on be free and eat the sweetest grass and drink the purest water and be fanned by cool breezes from every direction."

THE BODHISATTVA HAD reached his twenty-ninth year, and his wife Yashodhara was with child. But he was now thinking in earnest of leaving home. Old age, sickness, and death, and the suffering that seemed to be everywhere, cast restrictions on existence that he could not accept as final. Somehow he had to triumph over these enemies of happiness. Yet he could not hope to do so by whiling away his life in the palace. His encounter with the mendicant seemed to show the path he must follow to come to grips with these profound vexations.

As he later explained, "Before my enlightenment, while I was still only an unenlightened bodhisattva, being myself subject to birth, aging, ailment, death, sorrow and defilement, I sought after what was also subject to these things. Then I thought: Why, being myself subject to birth, aging, ailment, death, sorrow and defilement, do I seek after what is also subject to these things? Suppose, being myself subject to these things, seeing danger in them, I sought after the unborn, unaging, unailing, deathless, sorrowless, undefiled supreme surcease of bondage, nirvana?"[3]

And again: "Before my enlightenment, while I was still only an unenlightened bodhisattva, I thought: House life is crowded and dusty; life gone forth is wide open. It is not easy, living in a household, to lead a holy life as utterly perfect and pure as a polished shell. Suppose I shaved off my hair and beard, put on the yellow cloth, and went forth from the house life into homelessness."[4]

One night in the women's quarters, after an evening of entertainment, the prince woke up, and in the still-flickering lamplight saw the beautiful women lying about him, asleep in various positions of abandon. One young woman, who still held her lute, lay drooling from one side of her open mouth and snoring loudly. Other women lay propped against the walls or against pieces of furniture. Some had wine stains on their clothing. Others with their rich costumes thrown open lay in ungainly postures with their bodies exposed. In the stupor of sleep, they looked like randomly heaped corpses. The seductive vision of their beauty, which had so long captivated the prince, was shattered.

That same night, Yashodhara had a dream that Siddhartha had left her. She awoke and told him the dream. Then she said, "Lord, wherever you go, please take me with you." And thinking that he was going to a place beyond suffering and death, he agreed, and told her, "Where I go, you may go too."

Soon a son was born to Yashodhara and Siddhartha. Siddhartha gave the boy the name Rahula, which means "fetter."

It was a night not too long after the birth on which the bodhisattva chose to quit the palace forever and enter the path of homelessness. He decided to have a last look at his son Rahula before leaving. He found him asleep next to Yashodhara, with her hand resting lightly on his head. He knew that if he picked the baby up, he would wake his wife and leaving would become difficult. He turned on the spot, vowing to see his son again after he had attained enlightenment. All the palace women and all the guards and their captains, even those on watch, seemed to be sleeping soundly, for no one appeared to hinder his departure. The bodhisattva woke the charioteer Chandaka, commanded him to saddle his favorite horse, Kanthaka, and to accompany him on foot.

Legend recounts that in sympathy with Siddhartha's departure from the palace, this decisive step toward buddhahood, the gods cast a stupor over the palace. Kanthaka silenced his own neighing, and gods supported his hooves in their hands so that they made no noise on the paving stones. The gods it was also who opened the locked gates and swung them silently on their hinges, allowing the bodhisattva to depart unheard.

It was the full-moon night of the summer month of Ashadha when the bodhisattva, astride Kanthaka and with Chandaka at his heels, left Kapalivastu and struck out south through the forest. He was twenty-nine years old.

2

Homelessness, Teachers, Asceticism

REACHING THE TOP OF A HILL outside Kapilavastu, the bodhisattva considered turning to have a last look in the light of the moon at the city where he had spent his life. He had just firmly resolved to continue without looking back, when Mara, the embodiment of self-deception, appeared suspended in the air before him.

"Do not go," cried Mara, "for in seven days the golden wheel of universal sovereignty will appear, and you will become ruler over the whole world with its four great continents and myriads of islands."

"Mara! I know you!" exclaimed the bodhisattva. "And well I know that what you have said is true. But rulership over this world is not what I seek, but to become a buddha in order to heal its suffering."

Having been seen for what he was, Mara disappeared, but from that time on he clung to the bodhisattva like a shadow, waiting for the moment when weakness might appear.

The bodhisattva continued riding through the night and put a great distance between himself and Kapilavastu. In the morning he crossed a small river and dismounted on the far bank.

"Chandaka," he said, "I am entering the life of homelessness in order to seek truth for the sake of all. It is time for you to take Kanthaka and go back to Kapilavastu and my father." He handed his horse's bridle to the

trusted servant. Then he took off his gold and jewel ornaments, including the royal diadem from his head, and gave them also to Chandaka to
bring back.

Chandaka pleaded with the prince to give up his plan and return to
the palace. He spoke of the grief his departure would cause his father
and mother, his wife and child, his female attendants, his servants,
and Chandaka himself. He spoke of the disappointment of all the
Shakyans, his future subjects. But Siddhartha was firm. He took
Chandaka's sword and cut off his long hair, which was gathered on
top of his head in a princely coif. Then his attention fell on his robe of
fine embroidered silk, and he thought how ill-suited it was for a
wandering mendicant. He was puzzling over what alternative might
be possible when a deer hunter stepped out of the forest onto the
riverbank. He was wearing a simple saffron-dyed robe much like those
worn by wandering mendicants. The bodhisattva greeted the hunter
and offered to exchange clothing with him. The man was well pleased
and soon departed in the prince's rich robe, while the bodhisattva,
equally pleased, remained behind in the plain one. There was nothing to distinguish him now from an ordinary mendicant other than his
lordly bearing and beauty of face and limb. Only a seer or a rare
brahmin might have recognized the thirty-two major and eighty minor
marks he bore upon him.

"Now go back and tell the king what you have seen," the bodhisattva
told Chandaka.

But Chandaka found it extremely difficult to leave his lord alone and
unattended. Now he pleaded to be allowed to remain and enter homelessness with him. The bodhisattva replied that the time was not yet ripe
for him to enter such a life and firmly requested him finally to go do as
he was bidden. Chandaka turned away weeping, leading the horse.
Kanthaka now also sensed the parting. As he was being pulled away, he
whickered to his master and tried to stand his ground. At last Chandaka,
himself confused, managed to turn him, and the two crossed the river
and disappeared into the forest. It is said that Kanthaka was unable to

bear separation from his beloved master and died on the homeward journey, leaving Chandaka with a double sorrow to bear.

NOW THE BODHISATTVA had gone from prince to beggar in an instant. He had won the life he had contemplated with longing. Freedom was his; all worldly bonds had been severed. But now he must face the raw and rugged challenges of survival, and never before had he ever had even to bathe or dress by himself. He was supported only by the knowledge that this was the course he had to follow if he meant to be victorious over birth, old age, sickness, and death. He resolved never to turn back until he had accomplished this victory, and he began his wandering.

Day by day he learned to beg food. At first, accustomed as he was to only the finest dishes, he was nearly unable to put the leftovers of crude fare he collected in his alms bowl to his lips. But gradually he became used to this coarse food and to sleeping on the ground with no shelter but trees or rocks.

As the bodhisattva wandered, it began to dawn on him that he would eventually have to find a teacher. It had not suited his father to provide him with extensive training in philosophy or meditation; thus he felt he had to learn what could be learned from spiritual teachers. He soon discovered that, as there were many wandering mendicants pursuing the holy life of homelessness, there were also many teachers professing the various doctrines and different methods of practice that the mendicants followed. The teachers lived in forest or countryside as hermits or as heads of mendicant communities, usually close to towns or villages where food could be begged. For their part, the people were used to mendicants. It was traditionally regarded as a good deed to provide them with the minimal sustenance they required to pursue their spiritual strivings.

The mendicant Gautama made his way south by stages across the Ganges to the country of the Magadhans. There he took to staying in a cave on Mount Pandava in the neighborhood of the Magadhan capital Rajagriha.

As he made his morning begging rounds in the city, Gautama made a strong impression on the townsfolk. His stately carriage and elegant speech, his fine hands and regal gestures, were not in keeping with the rough robe he wore or his beggarly station. Also his directness, his intense and beautiful face, and the quality of his composure compelled attention. As he went about the city gathering alms food, crowds, each day larger, gathered to bow to him with joined hands or merely to stare as he passed.

Word of the singular mendicant came to the king of Magadha, Bimbisara. Then one morning the king stood on the palace roof looking down upon the city, and he himself caught a glimpse of the bodhisattva. He was profoundly struck by the sight of him and immediately sent messengers to follow him and find out where he was staying. The messengers followed Gautama across fields and through groves until they came to the slopes of Mount Pandava. There they saw the bodhisattva sit down in front of his cave and, after suitably arranging his seat, slowly eat his meal. They saw him wash his hands and bowl in a nearby stream and then afterward remain sitting cross-legged in front of the cave in meditation. Then they returned to the king and reported what they had seen.

The king set out at once by road for Mount Pandava in his chariot, accompanied by his retinue. When he got there, encumbered though he was by his royal robes and ornaments, he did not hesitate to climb the slopes until he came to the bodhisattva's cave. Seeing the beautiful young man with broad chest and strong arms sitting there deeply composed in meditation, the king was moved again. He approached the bodhisattva and greeted him respectfully. Then he took a seat on a nearby rock. The king courteously inquired about the mendicant's health, and Gautama, responding with due form, asked suitable questions concerning the king's own welfare.

When the proprieties had been observed, Bimbisara said, "I can tell from your bearing and demeanor as well as from your speech that you are no ordinary mendicant seeker. You could only be the scion of some noble and wealthy family. How is it that you have gone forth into homelessness while still so young? It is understandable and proper for a householder to abandon his responsibilities and seek the eternal verities when he has reached a certain age, when he has fulfilled his familial duties and his children are grown. Perhaps you have gone forth in the prime of manhood because some trouble has driven you. Or perhaps you are impatient and do not wish to wait long years for your inheritance. If either of those is the case, I stand ready here and now to offer you half my kingdom. For my eye sees clearly that you are suited to high estate and rulership. Why should one born to command men be wandering about as a homeless beggar? Or if you have been wronged by your own kin or driven out of your home, I am fully prepared to stand with you at the head of my armies. We shall conquer what is rightfully yours."

"Sir, you are kind," replied the bodhisattva. "But I have no need of your kingdom or your armies. Of my own accord I have left behind a great and prosperous kingdom. My father is Shuddhodana, son of the noble Gautama clan and king of the Shakyans in Kapilavastu. I have entered homelessness because I cannot accept the tyranny of sickness, old age, and death. These are the enemies I yearn to conquer. Against them your armies are powerless. Only through spiritual striving may I find a way to raise the victory banner against these ravagers of happiness. This is the goal I seek, and nothing can turn me aside from it. As to waiting till later, who knows how long one may live?"

King Bimbisara admired the young man none the less for having rejected both his generosity and his advice. He felt the conviction and wisdom in his words and was directly touched by them, realizing that he too was in no way proof against impermanence.

"Since I cannot dissuade you," he said, "my wish is that you may attain your great goal quickly and without obstruction. And when you do, please show me your favor and return to my country, and let my subjects and me benefit from your wisdom."

Gautama agreed to this, and the king arose and courteously took his leave.

SOON AFTER THIS, having heard of a highly reputed teacher, the bodhisattva traveled back north across the Ganges to the hermitage of the renowned sage Arada of the Kalama clan, not far from the city of Vaishali. When he got there he found that Arada had a large community of followers living round about him in the forest. Without hesitation, Gautama asked to see the teacher. One of the disciples conducted him into Master Arada's presence.

"Sir," said Gautama, "I wish to lead a holy life under your guidance. Please allow me to remain here and teach me your doctrine and practice."

Arada looked the bodhisattva over appraisingly and was impressed by what he saw. "Young man," he replied, "you may stay and be my student. My doctrine is such that a wise person may quickly learn it. Having learned it, he can enter upon the practice of it. Practicing it in meditation, he can quickly attain the knowledge possessed by his teacher through his own direct realization."

The bodhisattva explained to Arada how he had been shocked by the sight of old age, sickness, and death, and deeply troubled by the realization that whatever is born must always suffer from impermanence and sooner or later die. How frail and meaningless happiness had become! He had realized he must search to make a relationship with something that lay beyond birth, old age, sickness, and death. Yet all interests, desires, ambitions, and strivings—the very life of the senses itself—only seemed to draw one further into the cycle of existence.

Arada replied that Gautama's insight was accurate and explained his metaphysical views about an eternal principle lying beyond the world of the senses. Gautama quickly learned Arada's doctrine in detail. When he was able to recite it flawlessly and answer questions about it correctly, Arada gave him the instructions he needed to attain successive levels of meditative absorption.

The practice began with physical seclusion from distractions of the senses — going to a quiet place. Then it was necessary to withdraw the mind's attention from the tyranny of desire and aversion, lethargy and restlessness, attachment and doubt — all those factors that keep one caught up in the drama of the phenomenal world. Once Gautama had accomplished this, he experienced freedom from distraction by sense consciousness and the joy arising from this freedom, as well as a sense of physical well-being. But this state still had to be maintained through thoughts. In the next level of meditation, the guidance of thoughts fell away, and there was the new joy of unwavering concentration as well as of the physical well-being. In the third level, joy was recognized as an obstacle. Gautama attained a meditative absorption where there was neither joy nor suffering, only alertness and well-being. Finally even the solidity of well-being became too coarse, and only unperturbed wakefulness remained.

The bodhisattva was able to progress through these four levels of meditation with unusual swiftness. Sometimes he was able to move on to the next step without having Arada explain it to him. Then at last he went to the teacher, who told him, "These four levels of meditative absorption have taken you beyond material form. Still there are subtle levels beyond form that hold one a prisoner in the cycle of suffering. I will teach you how to rise above these."

Arada taught Gautama that he first had to free his meditative awareness from lingering attachment to the subtle form of an object. To do this, he must enter absorption upon that subtle form and then shift his awareness out beyond its boundaries. In this way he could attain the absorption on boundless space. When that too was recognized as a clumsy fixation, he was to shift his awareness from boundless space to the consciousness perceiving it. This brought the absorption on boundless consciousness. The last phase that Arada could teach him was the meditative absorption based on emptiness, which came from letting awareness relinquish the emphasis on perception that remains as a vestige in boundless consciousness.

Gautama was not very long in achieving the absorption based on emptiness, and he went to Arada and told him of his accomplishment. Arada was deeply moved. He said to the bodhisattva, "I am very fortunate to have encountered a disciple as gifted as you. In a short time you have learned and directly realized everything I know myself. I have no more to teach you. Your spiritual realization is equal to mine. Why not remain here with us, and you and I together will lead this community?"

But Gautama still felt himself far from total liberation. The goal of enlightenment still lay before him. So he thanked Arada Kalama for all that he had taught him, and courteously took his leave.

GAUTAMA HAD HEARD of another well-known forest master by the name of Rudraka Ramaputra, whose community was not far away. He set out through the country and soon found his way there. He presented himself to the master and told him what he had learned and what he was seeking. Then he asked to receive Rudraka's teaching.

Rudraka's doctrine was more elaborate than Arada's but similar. The meditative practice also was along the same lines, but Rudraka had mastered one more level of meditation beyond that based on emptiness. This was the level of neither perception nor nonperception.

The absorption based on emptiness still contained an imbalance resulting from falling into emptiness by letting go of consciousness. The next absorption neither perceived a new object nor was it turning its attention away from any.

When Gautama, in a short time, had achieved this final level, he went to Rudraka and told him so. Rudraka declared that the young mendicant had now reached his own level of realization. Perceiving the intensity of Gautama's seeking mind and the clarity of his insight, Rudraka requested him to stay and take over sole leadership of the community.

Gautama was pleased with this honor, but he declined Rudraka's offer. He explained as follows. "Even though this doctrine and practice have great subtlety, still, even when one has reached the level of neither perception nor nonperception, although there is then liberation from form and from formlessness, there is still something left over — the thing that has been liberated from them, a watcher of "neither perception nor nonperception." As long as such a watcher, which some call a soul, remains, though one may momentarily be secluded from the cycle of suffering, the watcher remains as a seed for rebirth. As soon as the situation changes, rebirth easily takes place again. This is just what happens now when I get up from meditating. No matter how profound my absorption, after a short time I get caught up again in the world of the senses. The basic causes and conditions for rebirth have not been extinguished! Complete liberation has not been achieved! Enlightenment must still be sought!"

Having explained in this way, the bodhisattva took leave of Rudraka Ramaputra and again resumed his wandering. He felt now that there was no more he could learn from teachers. His two teachers had set his feet on the path, but now the time had come for him to direct his own journey. He was determined to spare no exertion to attain enlightenment, his final goal.

He began traveling southeast and again crossed the Ganges. Then he moved by short stages through the country of the Magadhans. In the wild, uninhabited lands, he was sometimes plagued by fear, the kind of fear one feels when alone in a remote place. Walking through the forest and suddenly hearing the loud snapping of a branch behind him, he experienced dread. When such things happened, he deliberately worked to defeat his fear. He refused to move a hairsbreadth from the spot where the fear struck or even to change his posture until he had overcome it. Gradually he became better at this and began to seek out frightening places. He visited forest shrines in the middle of the night where terror made his hair stand on end and his skin crawl. He would not move from the spot until he had confronted the fear and subdued it.

At last he came to the region of Uruvilva on the Nairanjana River, not far from the little town of Gaya, a place where he decided to settle down and work on his task in earnest. "There," he later recounted, "I saw an agreeable plot of ground, a delightful grove, a clear-flowing river with pleasant, smooth banks, and nearby a village as alms resort. I thought: This will serve for the struggle of a clansman who seeks the struggle."5

Since he had entered homelessness, all about him he had seen holy men performing ascetic practices such as holding the breath, fasting, or meditating under the midday sun within a circle of fire. These practices meant subjecting oneself to tremendous hardship and pain, which seemed to be a way to subdue oneself, to conquer completely the desires and attachments that made one get caught up again and again in the transient world of birth, old age, sickness, and death. Since Gautama had failed to attain enlightenment through the methods he had tried so far, he now felt he must try asceticism.

The Buddha later recalled these times to his disciples. "I thought: Suppose, with my teeth clenched and my tongue pressed against the roof of my mouth, I beat down, constrain, and crush my mind with my mind? Then, as a strong man might seize a weaker by the head or shoulders and beat him down, constrain him and crush him, so with my teeth clenched and my tongue pressed against the roof of my mouth, I beat down, constrained, and crushed my mind with my mind. Sweat ran from my armpits when I did so.

"Though tireless energy was aroused in me, and unremitting mindfulness established, yet my body was overwrought and uncalm because I was exhausted by the painful effort. But such painful feeling as arose in me gained no power over my mind.

"I thought: Suppose I practice the meditation that is without breathing? I stopped the in-breaths and out-breaths in my mouth and nose. When I did so, there was a loud sound of wind coming from my ear holes, as there is a loud sound when a smith's bellows are blown.

"I stopped the in-breaths and out-breaths in my mouth and nose and ears. When I did so, violent winds racked my head as if a strong man were splitting my head open with a sharp sword. And then there were violent pains in my head, as if a strong man were tightening a tough leather strap round my head as a head-band. And violent winds carved up my belly, as a clever butcher or his apprentice carves up an ox's belly with a sharp knife. And then there was a violent burning in my belly, as if two strong men had seized a weaker by both arms and were roasting him over a pit of live coals.

"And each time, though tireless energy was aroused in me and unremitting mindfulness established, yet my body was overwrought and uncalm because I was exhausted by the painful effort. But such painful feeling as arose in me gained no power over my mind. . . .

"I thought: Suppose I take very little food, say, a handful each time, whether it is bean soup or lentil soup or pea soup? I did so. And as I did so, my body reached a state of extreme emaciation; my limbs became like the joined segments of vine stems or bamboo stems, because of eating so little. My backside became like a camel's hoof; the projections of my spine stood forth like corded beads; my ribs jutted out as gaunt as the crazy rafters of an old roofless barn; the gleam of my eyes, sunk far down in their sockets, looked like the gleam of water sunk far down in a deep well; my scalp shriveled and withered as a green gourd shrivels and withers in the wind and sun. If I touched my belly skin, I encountered my backbone too; and if I touched my backbone, I encountered my belly skin too; for my belly skin cleaved to my backbone. If I made water or evacuated my bowels, I fell over on my face there. If I tried to ease my body by rubbing my limbs with my hands, the hair, rotted at its roots, fell away from my body, because of eating so little."

Gautama continued for a long time to mortify himself through extreme hardship. In the course of this time, Mara frequently came to him and tried to arouse the fear of death in him. He spoke sweetly to Gautama of the goodness of life and of the merit an active life in the world could bring — if only he would abandon the practices that were endangering his life. Gautama always replied firmly that he cared nothing for mere survival, especially since it was impossible anyhow. He did not fear death; he was willing to sacrifice his life. He sought only liberation from life and death.

Word of Gautama's activities had spread through the country among the mendicant seekers. They told one another how the former prince had quickly equaled Arada and Rudraka but then declined leadership of their communities. Especially they told of how he had now given himself over to the most relentless extremes of asceticism imaginable and must soon attain liberation or die. Kaundinya, the young brahmin who had predicted at the time of his birth that he would become a buddha and who had long since entered homelessness himself, heard of these things, and he came to find Gautama. He brought with him four fellow seekers named Ashvajit, Vashpa, Mahanaman, and Bhadrika. These five became Gautama's followers, and they served him. They brought him his tiny pittances of food. When he was too weak to drink, they helped him drink. When he was too weak to wash himself, they helped him wash. When he was too weak to stand, they helped him stand. And they awaited the day when he would attain enlightenment and be able to guide them also to the goal.

3

Enlightenment

AFTER NEARLY SIX YEARS had passed in this way, Gautama was close to death. He also began to wonder whether he had gone as far as it was possible to go in the direction of self-mortification. Whatever extremes of pain and privation others had ever suffered through asceticism, he had now suffered too. Others might possibly have equaled his own sufferings, but they could not have surpassed them. He had traveled that path as far as it could go. That method had been fully explored. Yet he had not succeeded in lifting himself beyond the ordinary human state. Supreme knowledge and vision still remained beyond his grasp.

Might there be another way of attaining enlightenment?

He remembered the incident in his childhood, at the plowing festival, when he had spontaneously entered meditation. As he later recalled, "I thought of the time when my Shakyan father was working and I was sitting in the cool shade of a rose-apple tree: quite secluded from sensual desires, secluded from unprofitable things I had entered upon and abode in the first meditation, which is accompanied by thinking and exploring with happiness and pleasure born of seclusion. I thought: Might that be the way to enlightenment? Then, following upon that memory there came the recognition that this was the way to enlightenment."[6]

Why should he be afraid, he wondered, of the pleasure he had experienced then in meditation? It was pleasure that had nothing to do with sensual desires or attachment to impermanent things. He came to the conclusion that there was no reason to shy away from pleasure and well-being that came from being firmly established in a meditative state.

And then he thought he could not attain that spontaneous pleasure in his extreme state of deprivation and weakness. He thought, "What if I should eat some rice and bread?"

So the bodhisattva ate some rice and bread. Kaundinya and his other four followers were disgusted, thinking he had given up the struggle and was indulging himself. Nevertheless, over the next days, he resumed taking one meager meal per day. His followers would have nothing to do with this, and they left him. Since he was still too weak to gather alms himself, young women from the village, who felt both pity and awe for him, brought him a little food each day. His strength and his fine radiant color began to return.

On the morning of the full-moon day of the spring month of Vaishakha, thirty-five years to the day after he was born, the bodhisattva made his way to the nearby Nairanjana River to bathe. Afterward he climbed out on the bank and sat down in a grove of trees. He was still a little weak but he was full of confidence. The night before he had had five auspicious dreams, and he was now certain that his goal could no longer elude him. He had dreamed that he was of immense size and the earth was his bed. The Himalayas were his pillow, and his left hand lay in the ocean on the east and his right hand in the ocean on the west. This he understood to mean that he would attain complete enlighten-ment. Then he had dreamed that a creeper sprouted out of his navel and grew high enough to touch the clouds. This he understood to mean that he would know the way to enlightenment. He had dreamed that little white insects with black heads covered his lower legs all the way up to his knees. This he thought betokened myriads of white-robed lay followers. He dreamed that birds of four colors came from the four directions, and then they landed at his feet and all turned white. This he understood to mean that people of all four castes — priests, warriors, merchants, and servants — would attain enlightenment through his teaching. Lastly, he dreamed that he was walking on a mountain of dirt but did not himself get dirty. This meant that all his material needs would be met, but through understanding their purpose he would never become attached to them.

As he was sitting there, a young and beautiful dark-haired woman wearing a dress of dark blue cloth approached. Her name was Sujata. She was the daughter of the chief cowherder of the village. Sujata too had heard that the mendicant Gautama was once again taking food. Now out of regard for Gautama, but also because she was hoping to win the gods' favor so they would bring her a suitable husband, she had decided to make a special food offering to the noble-born ascetic. Taking the finest cream that could be gotten from the milk of her father's herds, she had boiled some rice for him, sweetened it with wild honey, and put it in the finest dish she could find in her house. Now she bowed with respect and awe and requested him to accept her offering. Gautama smiled and took the dish of rice. Hardly daring to look at him, Sujata bowed again and departed.

Gautama ate the delicious food, the best food he had had since leaving the palace. It made him feel strong and good. Then he rested in the grove until the heat of the day had passed. Toward evening he was pervaded by a strong sense of purpose. He was sure that the time had come for the accomplishment of his task. He got up and crossed the river. On the other side, he met a grass-cutter who gave him some tufts of soft kusha grass. He walked on until he came to a place that felt suitable, and there he made a seat with the kusha grass on the east side of a pipal tree. It is said that this was the same place where countless buddhas before him had attained buddhahood. Then Gautama swore a resolute oath not to stir from that seat until he had attained enlightenment, even at the cost of his life.

As Gautama settled firmly into the cross-legged meditation posture,

Mara too realized that the crucial moment had come, and he trembled. He knew that once the bodhisattva had attained enlightenment, he would be forever beyond his power. The bodhisattva would also lead countless others beyond his power, and his realm would be depleted. By fear, by delusion, by desire, by discontent, by resentment, by doubt, by confusion — by some means such as these he must shatter the bodhisattva's resolve. He first approached the bodhisattva and sought to defeat him by simple intimidation. "Rise up, Siddhartha, kshatriya prince afraid of death. How dare you seat yourself in my seat. You have ventured where you surely do not belong! You overstep yourself, little man. Follow your proper path and give up the way of liberation. Look after your abandoned family and kingdom!"

The bodhisattva remained composed and payed Mara no heed.

Mara summoned his sons and daughters and his demon horde and held a council. Then he approached the bodhisattva in the guise of the god of love. He raised his bow of flowers strung with a line of humming bees and shot the bodhisattva with the arrow of desire. But the arrow hung in the air and fell harmlessly aside.

Then Mara mounted his war elephant and gathered his host. There were monsters and goblins of every description. Some had one head, some many. The comely ones had heads of animals such as crocodiles, snakes, or hyenas. Others had faces with no recognizable features that oozed like swollen pustules. Others had fang-filled mouths or eyes on their bellies or great pointed horns growing out of their joints. Some had gray skin with red spots, other scarlet hides sprouting long, crooked yellow spines. Some were tall as trees, other were huge and squat, and still others in swarms moved over every open space like rats. They brandished clubs, maces, spears, sharpened stakes, or other instruments of destruction. All at once they charged, loosing their weapons. Those who had no weapons hurled large jagged rocks. They bellowed hideously, emitted hoarse cries and terrifying screams. They screeched and howled, challenging the heavens with their din.

Before this onslaught, the bodhisattva remained unmoved, unper-

turbed. The weapons and projectiles either stayed suspended in the air
or fell harmlessly to the ground. Some, meeting the sweet peacefulness
of the bodhisattva's equanimity, were transformed into lotus petals,
which exuded a lovely fragrance and floated softly down.

Then Mara in desperation challenged the bodhisattva again, asking
him by what right he dared to occupy the seat that rightly belonged to
himself. He launched a whirlwind at Gautama, but not even the hem
of the bodhisattva's robe stirred. Mara sent a raging deluge, then
blinding sheets of fire. The bodhisattva remained untouched and
profoundly composed. Then he answered Mara's question. He declared that he had earned the right to that sacred seat through the
merit of countless lives of practicing generosity and the rest of the ten
transcendental virtues. "If you have any right to this seat," he challenged Mara, "then what witnesses do you have that you have practiced the ten virtues?"

Mara roared with laughter, and all of his misshapen creatures loudly
bawled out their testimony. Then he turned on the bodhisattva, thinking that now he had him because he was utterly alone. "What witnesses
do *you* have?" he lashed out.

The bodhisattva reached out and touched the earth with his finger-
tips. "The earth is my witness," he said. Then from very deep down
came an immense booming and rumbling from the shaking of the
very essence of the earth element itself. All the earth shook and its
thundering drowned out the terrified cries of Mara's minions. In a
moment the entire host had fled. Then Mara himself, defeated, slunk
away.

The bodhisattva had triumphed over Mara. The air cleared and was
still. The full moon rose in the sky and shone softly. The bodhisattva,
unmoving, entered into the first level of meditation. The night was
utterly silent, as even insects made no murmur. As the moon continued
to rise, the bodhisattva's composure deepened, and one by one he
mastered the levels of meditation until he reached the fourth. His
concentration was bright and unblemished, full and balanced. Then

through great confidence and trust, he relinquished the watcher, and his mind entered into a fathomless openness untroubled by content. Here the bodhisattva naturally rested until a profound contentment pervaded him. But as one who already knew the way, he did not become caught up in this. Rather, with utter clarity and tenderness, he turned his mind to untying the knot of birth, old age, sickness, and death.

He saw that the condition for old age, sickness, and death is birth. Once birth happens, the rest follows inevitably. He saw that the condition for birth lay in processes of becoming already set in motion; that the condition for this was grasping or craving; that the condition for this was desire; and the condition for desire, feelings of happiness, suffering, or indifference; and the condition for these, sensual contact; and the condition for sensual contact, the fields of the senses; the condition for sense fields, the arising of mind-body; the condition for mind-body, consciousness. He saw that mind-body and consciousness condition each other to make a rudimentary sense of self. He saw that the condition for consciousness was volitional impulses, and finally that the condition for volitional impulses was ignorance.

Thus he saw that the whole process ending in old age and death begins when basic intelligence slips into unawareness of its own nature. In this way all-pervading intelligence strays into the sense of a self.

After the bodhisattva had penetrated the nature of the process of birth, old age, sickness, and death, the clarity and openness of his mind increased yet further. Then in the first watch of the night, his inner vision became completely unobstructed. This is called the opening of the divine eye. Then he turned his attention to the past, and he saw his and others' countless past lives stretching back over many eons and ages of the world. Even back through world ages separated from the present one by long intervals of universal destruction, he knew that at a certain time he had been thus and such a person. He had been this kind of being, of this sex, of this race, had eaten this food, and had lived this long. Then he had been born again this or that way and once more lived through certain circumstances, and thus had been born and had died and been reborn again an incalculable number of times. This he saw in relation to himself and all other beings.

Then, in the second watch of the night, moved by compassion he opened his wisdom eye yet further and saw the spectacle of the whole universe as in a spotless mirror. He saw beings being born and passing away in accordance with karma, the laws of cause and effect. Just as, when one clears one's throat, one is next ready to speak, past deeds create a certain inclination. When the basic condition of ignorance is present, the inclination takes shape in a certain kind of volitional impulses, which engender a certain consciousness, and so on up to old age and death, and then once more into ignorance and volitional impulses. Seeing birth and death occurring in accordance with this chain of causality, the bodhisattva saw the cyclic paths of all beings. He saw the fortunate and the unfortunate, the exalted and the lowly going their various ways. He saw how, ignorant and suffering, they were tossed on the stormy waves of birth, old age, sickness, and death.

In the third and last watch of the night, he applied himself to the task of rooting out this suffering once and for all. He had clearly understood the wheel of dependent arising in which each stage follows from a preceding cause, beginning with ignorance. And he saw how beings were driven on it by the powerful motive force of karma. Now his divine eye sought the means of liberation. He saw that through the cessation of birth, old age and death would not exist; through the cessation of becoming, there would be no birth; through the cessation of grasping, no becoming — and so back through the sequence of causation to ignorance. He saw suffering, the cause of suffering, the cessation of suffering, and at last also the path to cessation.

At the end of the third watch, at the first light of dawn the bodhisattva saw through the very last trace of ignorance in himself. Thus he attained complete and utter enlightenment and became the Buddha. The first words that came to him were these:

Seeking but not finding the House Builder,
I traveled through the round of countless births:
O painful is birth ever and again.
　House Builder, you have now been seen;
　You shall not build the house again.
　Your rafters have been broken down;
　Your ridge pole is demolished too.
My mind has now attained the unformed nirvana
*And reached the end of every kind of craving.*7

Then he thought: "I have attained the unborn. My liberation is unassailable. This is my last birth. There will now be no renewal of becoming."

4

Turning the Wheel

FOLLOWING THE MOMENT of enlightenment the Buddha continued to sit at the root of the Bodhi (Enlightenment) Tree for seven days without moving, resting without thought in a state of well-being.

At the end of the seventh day, he emerged from that thoughtless state and began to consider again the insights that had led him to enlightenment. Each thing arises in dependence on a cause. He reviewed the sequence of causation, beginning with ignorance and ending in old age and death. This he understood again is how all the suffering and misery of beings arises. Knowing each thing to have its cause, he saw, is the first big step in eradicating all doubts.

In the second watch of the night, he again considered the sequence of dependent arising working backward from the effects to the causes, making it clear in his mind once more that by eliminating the causes of suffering, it is possible to bring about the cessation of all the suffering of beings. Knowing that cessation of the causes brings about cessation of the effects, he saw, is what completes the eradication of all doubts.

In the final watch of the night, he reconsidered the sequence of interdependent causes both forward and backward, from the points of view of both arising and cessation; and when he was fully satisfied with his understanding of this, he said:

When things are fully manifest
To the ardent meditating brahmin,
There, like the sun who lights the sky,
He stands repelling Mara's hosts.[8]

Then again he saw the panorama of existence with the divine eye, and he saw the whole world burning, since all the beings in it were burning with the fevers of passion, aggression, and delusion arising from ignorance and the sense of a self.

The Buddha spent another seven days meditating beneath a banyan tree not far away. At the end of that time, a brahmin with a proud and supercilious air approached the Blessed One, greeted him, and engaged him in polite conversation. When the amenities were finished, he asked him, "What is a brahmin, Master Gautama? What makes a brahmin a brahmin?"

The Buddha replied that since "brahmin" meant someone living a holy life, being a brahmin was not a matter of hereditary caste. "Anyone," he went on, "who has purified his mind and is humble is a brahmin. Only if he is not proud, is without arrogance, can he be called a brahmin."

The brahmin had nothing more to say. He rose and departed.

The Buddha moved to another place under a tree not far from where he had been sitting and again rested in meditation. Not long after, however, a tremendous unseasonal rainstorm arose, with cold winds and the rain coming down in sheets. "This storm is the work of Mara," thought the Blessed One as he faced the hardship it brought him. Then a great serpent, Muchalinda, king of the nagas, rose from his realm beneath the earth. He spread his hood above the Blessed One's head and wrapped his coils about his body. Thus the Blessed One was protected from rain, heat, cold, and biting insects. At the end of seven days, the rain passed. The naga then transformed into a brahmin youth, who bowed to the Buddha with palms joined, and departed.

During the time the Buddha was meditating in various places in the vicinity of the Bodhi Tree, once the thought occurred to him, "I am free from those useless ascetic practices. I am mindful and aware. I have attained enlightenment."

Mara was aware of the Buddha's thought and appeared, chiding: "You have abandoned the path of asceticism by which homeless ones purify themselves. You think you are pure, but in reality you are far from pure, and you have given up the means of purification!"

The Buddha at once recognized Mara and replied, "Ascetic practices are as irrelevant for gaining liberation as oars for moving over dry land. It is through discipline, meditation, and knowledge that I attained enlightenment. And now that I have done so, you, Mara, are forever beaten!"

Mara thought, "The Blessed One knows me!" and he vanished.

Another time the Blessed One thought, "It is not a good thing to live without anyone to look up to, follow, or take refuge in. But there is no holy teacher or brahmin, no one in this world, who surpasses me in discipline, meditation, or knowledge whom I could honor and venerate. All there is for me to honor and venerate is the Dharma, the holy Teaching that I have discovered myself." Then he thought, "That is good. I shall place myself under that. The enlightened buddhas of the past ages of the world also lived honoring and venerating the precious holy Dharma."

Now the Buddha thought whether he should teach the Dharma to others. "It is too profound and too difficult to be taught," he thought. "It runs too much against the grain of stubborn and all-pervasive delusion. Being in its essence beyond concept and thought, it is too subtle for even the wise to grasp. A world so totally caught up in attachment, so used to living in lust and aggression, has too much dust on its eyes ever to be able to perceive the truth that it hides from."

Thus the Blessed One concluded he would not teach. He would remain silent. He would simply rest in his illumination, since it would be futile to try to convey it to others.

Then the god Sahampati became aware of the Buddha's decision. He vanished from the heavenly realm of the brahma gods and appeared before the Blessed One. With one knee to the ground and his palms joined, Sahampati entreated the Blessed One on behalf of all beings to "turn the wheel of Dharma." He pleaded that there were many who were genuine seekers of the truth with but little dust on their eyes. These would be able to perceive the Dharma in its subtlety and depth. "If you will only teach," he said, "you will liberate countless beings from the cycle of suffering."

Having been entreated in this manner, the Buddha was moved by compassion. He consented to the god's request by remaining silent, and when he knew he had been heard, Sahampati bowed and departed.

In all the Buddha spent forty-nine days after his enlightenment meditating near the Bodhi Tree. At the end of this time, two wealthy merchants from the north, Trapusha and Bhallika, were passing on a nearby road with their train of wares. Some of their carts got stuck in the mud, and they were delayed. Walking about in the vicinity to pass the time, they caught sight of the Buddha meditating beneath a tree. They were struck by his majesty and radiant presence, so they determined to make him an offering. They got some rice cakes and honey from among their stores, which they returned and offered to the Buddha, bowing with respect.

The Blessed One thought to himself, "Tathagatas, perfected ones, do not accept alms in their hands," and made no motion. Then the four celestial kings who guard the four quarters of the world appeared and presented him with a bowl, saying, "Lord, please take the food in this." Then the Buddha received the rice cakes and honey from the two merchants in this bowl.

The merchants were wonderstruck. After the Buddha had spoken a few words to them, the two of them prostrated themselves and said, "We take refuge in the Buddha and the Dharma, his teaching."

These two were the first to declare themselves followers of the Buddha by "taking refuge." All later followers took a threefold refuge, the third refuge being in the Sangha, the community of followers. But at this time there was no Sangha.

After the merchants had gone their way, the Buddha ate the rice cakes and honey, thus breaking his forty-nine day fast.

The Tathagata then considered whom he might teach. The first who came to his mind were his two former teachers Arada Kalama and Rudraka Ramaputra. "Those two," he thought, "truly have little dust on their eyes." But as he deliberated this possibility, his divine eye revealed to him that these two venerable brahmins had died, the first a week ago and the second only the previous night. Then he thought again and concluded that the best course open to him was to try to transmit his understanding to those five erstwhile followers of his who had deserted him when he had begun to eat again after his years of starvation. He knew them to be staying at the Deer Park, or Rishivadana, near Varanasi, a place frequented by many mendicant seekers.

Having now remained by the Bodhi Tree near Gaya in the region of Uruvilva as long as he chose, the Blessed One started north for Varanasi. One day on the road, he met a naked ascetic by the name of Upaka, who was struck by the Buddha's serenity and radiance.

"Friend," said Upaka, "anyone with eyes can see that you are highly accomplished spiritually. Who is your teacher and what dharma do you follow?"

The Buddha replied, "I have transcended all existence and become omniscient. My insight is unobstructed, and I am liberated from all desire. I have achieved this on my own, without a teacher. Because I alone in the world am completely enlightened, I myself am the world's teacher. Extinguished are all my passions, all my obscurations, gone. I am now on my way to the capital of the Kashis to turn the wheel of the true Dharma. In a world of the blind, I shall beat the great drum of Dharma."

"So you claim to be a victorious one, a jina?" Upaka asked.

"If a jina is one," said the Buddha, "whose defilements and obscurations are completely exhausted and who sees things as they are with unimpaired clarity, then that may be said of me."

"Well," said Upaka, shaking his head, "I hope you're right." And he continued on his wandering, taking a side road.

AFTER A FEW days, having crossed the Ganges, the Blessed One arrived at the Deer Park not far from Varanasi. The group of his five former disciples who were sitting there saw him coming. They quickly agreed among themselves that since he was a backslider from the true path, they should not show him any deference. Still they thought that out of politeness, they could at least prepare him a seat and let him sit with them. But when he approached them, his presence was so overwhelming that they were unable to hold themselves back. One of them hopped up to take his blanket and bowl, another arranged his seat, and a third fetched water so that he could wash his feet.

So the Blessed One sat down on the seat they had prepared for him and washed his feet. When they began talking, however, the five still refused to address him in honorific terms. They called him "friend" and "Gautama."

"Bhikshus [mendicant or monk]," he said, "do not address a Tathagata by name and as 'friend': such a one has completed the task and is fully enlightened. Listen, bhikshus, the unborn, the deathless, has been attained. I shall teach you. I shall instruct you in the true Dharma. If you practice according to my instructions, you will be able to realize it yourselves through your own direct knowledge. You will achieve the goal of the holy life for the sake of which clansmen rightly leave the householder's life and enter homelessness."

But the five said, "Now, Gautama, you know well that even though you practiced extreme austerities, you never attained any particular exalted state beyond the human level. You may have advanced beyond us, but then you gave up what you had gained. Now you carry on indulging yourself and living as you please. How do you expect us to believe that you have attained the ultimate goal?"

"Listen," the Buddha told the five, "a Tathagata is not self-indulgent, nor does he give up the struggle." Then he repeated his words, exhorting them to listen to the Dharma. A second time, the five gave their skeptical answer. A third time, the Blessed One exhorted them in the same terms: "The unborn, the deathless, has been attained. I shall teach you. I shall instruct you in the true Dharma." A third time, they answered as before.

Then he asked them if they had ever known him to speak like this before.

"No, lord," they admitted.

Then he proposed yet a fourth time to teach them the Dharma. At last, in the face of his unwavering insistence, they yielded and agreed to at least listen.

First he explained to the five mendicants led by Kaundinya that there are two extremes to be refrained from rather than cultivated. "What two? There is devotion to the pursuit of pleasure in sensual desires, which is low, coarse, vulgar, ignoble, and harmful; and second, there is devotion to self-mortification, which is painful, ignoble, and harmful." Then he explained that he had discovered a middle way: "The middle way discovered by a Tathagata avoids both these extremes; it gives vision, gives knowledge, and leads to peace, to direct knowledge, to enlightenment, to nirvana. And what is the middle way? It is the Noble Eightfold Path, that is to say: right view, right intention, right speech, right action, right livelihood, right effort, right mindfulness, right concentration."9

In this first of his talks on the Dharma, the Buddha taught not only the Eightfold Path but also the Four Noble Truths. He said: "There is this Noble Truth of suffering: Birth is suffering, aging is suffering, sickness is suffering, death is suffering, sorrow and lamentation, pain, grief, and despair are suffering, association with the loathed is suffering, dissociation from the loved is suffering, not to get what one wants is suffering. . . .

"There is this Noble Truth of the origin of suffering: It is craving, which produces renewal of being, is accompanied by relish and lust, relishing this and that; in other words, craving for sensual desires, craving for being, craving for nonbeing.

"There is this Noble Truth of the cessation of suffering: It is the remainderless fading and ceasing, the giving up, relinquishing, letting go, and rejecting of that same craving.

"There is this Noble Truth of the way leading to the cessation of suffering: It is this Noble Eightfold Path, that is to say: right view, right intention, right speech, right action, right livelihood, right effort, right mindfulness, and right concentration."[10]

He explained that the truth of suffering had to be penetrated by fully understanding suffering. As for the truth of the origin of suffering, one has to abandon that origin. The truth of the cessation of suffering means realizing that the cessation of suffering is really possible, and to achieve that cessation one has to cultivate the Eightfold Path. He explained that he had achieved enlightenment by fully realizing these Four Noble Truths.

As the Blessed One was explaining these things, a pure vision of the Dharma arose in Kaundinya. He realized that all that is subject to arising is subject to cessation. And the Blessed One exclaimed, "Kaundinya knows! Kaundinya knows!"

And indeed Kaundinya's doubts had vanished. As he listened to the words of the Blessed One, perfect confidence based on his own direct knowledge had arisen. He had acquired that kind of independent knowledge that no longer requires confirmation from someone else, no longer needs to be further tested.

Then Kaundinya asked the Buddha to accept him formally as his disciple. So the Buddha gave him ordination as a bhikshu, or monk, in the order of mendicants headed by himself. He did this simply by saying: "Come, bhikshu. The Dharma has been properly proclaimed. Live the holy life for the complete ending of suffering."

Then the Blessed One instructed the four others further, and after a short time, there arose in them also a pure vision of the Dharma. They also clearly saw that all that is subject to arising is subject to cessation. They too asked to be accepted into the Buddha's order, and the Buddha ordained them in the same way as he had ordained Kaundinya.

THE MORNING AFTER this first turning of the wheel of Dharma, the Buddha and his disciples went to gather alms food. Soon, however, they discovered that all six of them were able to live on the food brought back by three.

The Buddha continued teaching in the Deer Park. Listening to him day after day, his first five disciples attained a first, then a second, a third, and finally a fourth level of realization. Thus they became arhats, "enemy destroyers," those who have destroyed within themselves all the obstacles to enlightenment.

There were many others in the Deer Park who were trying to understand how to lead the holy life, and many of them also began listening to the Buddha.

During this period, the Blessed One gave the teaching on nonself, or non-ego. The idea of an eternal self, an ego or soul, connected with an eternal divine principle in the universe and transmigrating from rebirth to rebirth, was a central tenet of Hinduism. The Buddha taught that there is no such self, but only the illusion of a self. If a real self did exist, he explained, it would only be a cause of suffering, and if it were eternal it would be a cause of suffering that could never be removed. That eternal self would enter again and again into the web of experience, into the cycle of rebirth. Then there would be no Third Noble Truth of the cessation of suffering and thus no enlightenment. As it is, he taught, there is only an illusion of a self, but even that is enough to function as the principal obstacle to liberation, to the cessation of suffering.

But the obstacle of an illusory self, taught the Tathagata, who was fresh from victory, falls away when it is seen as it is. Rather than being a solid, eternal entity, it is merely a temporary composite of form, feeling, perception, conceptual formations, and consciousness, which are called the five skandhas, or aggregates. Rather than a definite self to cling to, and which in turn clings to other things, there is just an ever-

shifting mosaic composed of those five aggregates. Once this is recognized, one becomes dispassionate toward what one formerly clung to.
Desire fades away, and the heart is liberated. Nothing remains that is
subject to the round of suffering and rebirth.

IN VARANASI at this time, there lived a rich merchant's son named
Yasha. He had been raised in a manner recalling the Buddha's own
youth. He spent his life in his father's palaces, where he was sheltered
and protected, provided with many servants, and surrounded by a
multitude of female attendants skilled in entertaining him and fulfill-
ing his every desire. One night not long after the Buddha had begun
turning the wheel of Dharma in the Deer Park, Yasha awoke in the
middle of the night and beheld about him, as the Buddha had, the
dissolute spectacle of sleeping bodies in unbecoming disarray, and he
experienced profound revulsion. He was instantly so thoroughly disgusted and horrified with himself and the life he was leading that then
and there he fled from the palace, still wearing his golden bedroom
slippers.

Yasha made his way in the darkness out of the city gates and through
the countryside to Rishivadana and the Deer Park. It was one of the
occasions when the Buddha had risen in the darkness before dawn and
was pacing back and forth in the open. He saw Yasha coming, and when
the youth was quite close, he heard him say, "This is terrifying, this is
horrid!" And the Buddha said, "Here there is nothing terrifying or
horrid, Yasha. Come have a seat, and I will teach you the Dharma."

Yasha at once felt a sense of comfort and hope. He took off his golden
slippers, prostrated to the Tathagata, and sat down off to one side. First
the Buddha gave him ordinary spiritual instruction on generosity and
virtue and the abandonment of overindulgence in sensual pleasures.
But then, as he saw Yasha's mind growing calmer and more open, he
began to speak to him of the more central insights he had discovered
beneath the Bodhi Tree. Yasha soaked up the Blessed One's words and
meaning as clean, undyed cloth soaks up dye, and as he sat there, a

clear and perfect vision of the Dharma arose in him: all that is subject to arising is subject to cessation.

Around this time Yasha's absence from the palace was noticed and reported to his father. The merchant sent out men in all directions to hunt for him, and he himself went to the Deer Park to look. Seeing him coming, the Buddha used his supernormal powers to make Yasha invisible to the merchant. The merchant approached and respectfully inquired of the Blessed One if he had seen his son. The Buddha responded by inviting him to sit down with him for a moment, suggesting that if he did, he might well see the lad. The merchant thought this was a good idea, so he prostrated himself to the Blessed One and sat down off to one side. Then the Buddha started teaching him much in the same way as he had Yasha. Soon the wealthy merchant began to comprehend the Dharma, and in no long time he penetrated to the heart of it and developed independent understanding of it through direct realization. He was thrilled and full of gratitude, and he exclaimed, "This is truly magnificent, Lord. You have spoken so lucidly and made the nature of things as they really are so clear that even a person like myself, caught up in matters of commerce and wealth, was able to see it for myself. I take refuge in the Blessed One, I take refuge in the Dharma, and I take refuge in the Sangha of bhikshus. From today on, please regard me as your follower who takes refuge in you for as long as I live."

In this way the wealthy merchant became the first follower of the Buddha to take the triple refuge.

Meanwhile, Yasha was sitting to one side, listening. As he heard the Blessed One explain the Dharma again, clinging fell away, and he became free of all defilements that obscure the mind. This is tantamount to the realization of an arhat. The Buddha then made him visible to the merchant once more. When the merchant saw him, he said, "Yasha, my son! How glad I am to find you. But now your mother is beside herself with grief. Please think of her suffering and return home!"

But the Blessed One interceded. He said, "Suppose Yasha has penetrated to the heart of the Dharma the way you have and seen that
profound truth without veils, and then on top of that, through lack of
clinging, all defilements have been purified in him — do you think he
will be able to go back to the palace and continue to lead a householder's life just as he did before?"

"I suppose not, lord," admitted the merchant. "No, he could not go
on as before. I suppose we must lose him. But though we do, I see it is
definitely for the better. In truth, it is wonderful. So in that case, let me
simply request that you receive your meal of the day from me at my
house, and bring Yasha along as your attendant."

The Blessed One expressed his consent by remaining silent. Then
the merchant left, and Yasha asked the Buddha to admit him fully and
formally into the order as a bhikshu. The Buddha ordained him by
saying, "Come, bhikshu. The Dharma has been properly proclaimed.
Live the holy life for the complete ending of suffering." And then there
were seven arhats.

Morning had now arrived, so the Buddha dressed, took his bowl and
outer robe, and, accompanied by Yasha, who was now also clad as a
monk, went to the wealthy merchant's house to take the day's meal.
When he got there, he sat down on the seat that had been prepared for
him. Yasha's mother and wife greeted the Blessed One respectfully and
sat down on one side. Then he taught them the Dharma until they, too,
clearly saw that all that is subject to arising is subject to cessation.

The merchant and his wife served the Buddha and Yasha the meal
with their own hands, providing many excellent dishes. When the
Buddha had finished eating and had put down his bowl, they sat down
to one side, and the Buddha roused and encouraged them with further
talk of the Dharma. Then he rose from his seat and departed.

Not long after this, four of Yasha's friends, sons of leading merchant
families of Varanasi, heard that Yasha had shaved his head, donned
saffron-colored robes, and entered homelessness. When they heard this
they thought that it must have been really an extraordinary teacher and

teaching to have caused Yasha to do that. So they went to see the venerable Yasha. They bowed courteously with palms together and began asking questions. Yasha responded by taking them to see the Buddha. They prostrated to him and sat down off to one side, and he began to teach them. It was not long before an unblemished vision of the Dharma arose in their mind: that all that is subject to arising is subject to cessation. And as he taught them further, and because of absence of clinging, they were liberated from defilements. The Buddha ordained them by saying, "Come, bhikshus. The Dharma has been properly proclaimed. Live the holy life for the complete ending of suffering." And now there were eleven arhats.

Then fifty of Yasha's friends throughout that region, all sons of prominent or well-to-do families, also heard that Yasha had entered homelessness under the Buddha. They came to see him, and he conducted them to the Tathagata. After the Blessed One had instructed them for some time, they all also asked to be ordained as monks in his order, and the Buddha ordained them, saying "Come, bhikshus," and so on. And after he had taught them a while longer, they were liberated from defilements and became arhats, making now sixty-one in all.

The Buddha gathered all the arhats together, and said: "Bhikshus, I am free from all shackles, whether human or divine. You are free from all shackles, whether human or divine. Go now and wander for the welfare and happiness of many, out of compassion for the world, for the benefit, welfare, and happiness of gods and men. Teach the Dharma that is good in the beginning, good in the middle, and good in the end, both the words and the meaning. Explain a holy life that is utterly perfect and pure. There are beings with little dust on their eyes who will be lost through not hearing the Dharma. Some will understand the Dharma."[11] And he also told them: "As for myself, I have decided to go to Uruvilva in the Magadhan land to teach the Dharma." For he had remembered his promise to King Bimbisara.

Then Mara came and once more tried to dislodge the confidence of the Tathagata. He spoke to him harshly, saying, "You are bound by all the shackles, human and divine, especially the shackle in the air that has its hold upon the mind. Through that especially, I shall always keep you captive." But the Buddha, knowing who spoke and that his words were meaningless, paid him no heed. And when Mara knew he had been recognized, he vanished.

By now, the bhikshus whom the Blessed One had sent out had wandered in all directions and were beginning to bring in men who wanted to enter homelessness and be fully ordained as monks, members of the Sangha. It was becoming increasingly difficult to make arrangements for them all to come to the Buddha for this purpose. So the Buddha convoked an assembly of the bhikshus and authorized them all to grant both the entry into homelessness and the ordination. And he formulated exactly how it should be done.

First the entrant's hair and beard were to be shaved. Then the saffron-colored body cloth was to be put on and the upper robe arranged over one shoulder. The entrant then was to prostrate at the bhikshu's feet; then, kneeling, with the palms of the hands together, he was to repeat, "I take refuge in the Buddha, I take refuge in the Dharma, I take refuge in the Sangha" three times.

The Buddha also gave the assembled Sangha further teachings, in which he formulated doctrine and method more precisely than before and also gave some instructions for the organization of Sangha life.

In these times, when the Buddha was setting his Dharma and Sangha on a firm foundation, Mara frequently appeared, to try to shake his confidence — but always to no avail.

The Buddha spent the first rainy season after his enlightenment in the Deer Park near Varanasi. When he had remained there as long as he chose, he set off south for Uruvilva. One afternoon during the journey, he was passing the heat of the day meditating in a forest not far from the road. A pleasure outing had been going on in the woods nearby. Thirty young men who were friends had made an excursion to the forest with their wives. One unmarried man had brought a courtesan to accompany him. This courtesan had fled with some stolen property while her lover slept, and now the young men were crashing through the trees trying to find her when they came across the Buddha meditating at the foot of a tree.

"Lord," they said, "did you see a woman coming this way?"

"What are you lads up to with this woman?" the Buddha asked.

They told him the story, and he asked them, "What do you think? Is it better to be spending your time looking for this woman or looking for yourselves?"

"It's better to be looking for oneself, I suppose," they admitted.

"In that case, why don't you have a seat and I'll teach you the Dharma?"

So they all courteously prostrated to the Blessed One and sat down there among the trees. He began by teaching them straightforward things, such as generosity, which they could easily understand, and gradually led them to the core insights of the Buddha Dharma. After some time, a pure vision of the Buddha Dharma arose within them. They saw that everything subject to arising is also subject to cessation. Then they asked to enter homelessness and be ordained as monks, so the Blessed One said, "Come, bhikshus. The Dharma has been properly proclaimed. Live the holy life for the complete ending of suffering." And thus, before they left that little clearing in the forest, they all became venerable bhikshus.

THE BLESSED ONE continued walking through the country day by day until he reached the region of Uruvilva. In that region at the time there were three well-known holy men of the type who wore long hair, matted from never being washed or combed, piled up on top of their heads. These three were called Kashyapa of Uruvilva, Kashyapa of the River, and Kashyapa of Gaya. Some say they were brothers. In any case, the three Kashyapas counted as their followers five hundred, three hundred, and two hundred matted-hair ascetics, respectively, and theirs was the principal spiritual influence over the whole kingdom of Magadha at that time. The focal point of their practice was a ritual fire offering. In a chanted liturgy, practitioners made symbolic offerings to a deity supposed to be embodied in the flames and sought to invoke its powers.

The Buddha went to Kashyapa of Uruvilva and asked to spend the night in his fire-offering chamber, which was a dark cave. Kashyapa warned the Blessed One that there was a ferocious naga, or serpent deity, with supernormal powers living in the cave who would surely destroy him. For that reason, he said, he could not allow the Buddha to stay there. But the Blessed One insisted, repeating his request three times and saying that perhaps the naga would not be able to destroy him. Finally Kashyapa said, "Great monk, in that case you may stay there as long as you like."

The Blessed One entered the cave and, seating himself cross-legged in the middle of the fire-chamber floor, established himself in a meditative state. That alone enraged the naga, who manifested his anger by sending up clouds of smoke. The Buddha did not intend to harm the naga, so he simply countered the smoke with smoke. Then the naga emanated fire, which filled the cave. Thereupon the Buddha, entering into identification with the fire element, also raised fire, a great blaze that was enough to neutralize the naga's fire and singe him but leave skin and bone intact. Outside the night was lit up by the conflagration in the cave, whose flames raged from its mouth. The matted-hair ascetics standing around said to each other, "The great monk who is so beautiful is being destroyed by the naga."

In the morning the Blessed One came out of the cave with the reduced naga coiled harmlessly in his begging bowl. He said, "This is your naga, Kashyapa. His fire has been countered by fire." Kashyapa thought, "The great monk is very powerful, but he is not an arhat like me."

The Buddha went to stay in a nearby grove. During the night, he was visited by the four celestial kings who protect the four quarters of the world system. They stood like great lights at the four corners of his sleeping space and illuminated the whole wood. On his way to invite the Blessed One to the daily meal, Kashyapa saw the light and asked the Buddha about it. The Buddha told him, "Those were the four celestial kings. They came to me in the night for teaching." And Kashyapa thought, "The great monk is very powerful, but still he is not an arhat like me."

On succeeding nights, Brahma and Indra, chiefs of the gods, came to the Buddha in the same way for teaching. Kashyapa saw them also, but still he thought as before.

The time was coming for an important ritual at Kashyapa's hermitage that brought people from far and wide with gifts of food. It was a great occasion, a moment of glory for Kashyapa. The leader of the ascetics was dreading the Tathagata's appearance at the ritual, because he feared that the Buddha might perform some wonder that would leave Kashyapa himself looking less powerful before all his followers. Knowing this thought of Kashyapa's, on the day of the ritual the Tathagata went to a remote plane of the world system to gather alms and take his meal. The day following the great rite, when Kashyapa came to invite the Blessed One to the daily meal, he inquired about his absence on the previous day. "I was expecting you," he said, "and your seat and your food were prepared. Where were you?" The Buddha told him where he had gone and why. Again Kashyapa was profoundly impressed. "The great monk can see my thoughts so clearly!" he thought. But in his mind he still added, "He is not an arhat like me."

The Tathagata had a rag that needed to be washed. But in the grove where he was staying there was no water. Perceiving his need, the god Indra scooped out a pond there. At the edge of the pond he placed a large stone on which to beat the rag, and he also bent down the branch of a great tree so that the Buddha would have a place to hang the rag out to dry. Kashyapa came to invite the Blessed One to the daily meal. He saw all these things that had never been there before, and the Buddha explained to him what had happened. He thought, "Truly it is extraordinary that the great monk is served by the gods. But he is still not an arhat like me."

In the succeeding days, the Tathagata continued to perform various wonders, each more extraordinary than the last. These were witnessed by Kashyapa and often by the other matted-hair ascetics as well. Still Kashyapa remained stubbornly fixed in his view.

Around this time, the ascetics of the Kashyapa's community found that they could not split logs as they usually did to provide fuel for their ritual fires. No matter what they did, the logs would not split. They all thought, "This must be something the great monk is doing with his supernormal powers." Kashyapa had to go to the Buddha and ask him about it. The Blessed One asked him if he would like to have the logs split. When he said yes, suddenly all over the hermitage, the logs were split. Kashyapa thought, "What power the great monk has, that he could keep the logs from being split and then split them all at once. But still he is not an arhat like me."

On another occasion, there were heavy rains and a great flood inundated the low-lying areas, including the grove where the Buddha was staying. Kashyapa was afraid that the Tathagata had been washed away by the flood, so he went with some of his disciples in boats to see about him. The Buddha made the waters part and walked over to Kashyapa's boat on dry land. Then he rose up into the air, stayed suspended there for a moment, and then came down in Kashyapa's boat. Kashyapa thought, "The great monk is truly wondrous, since he is not subject even to the elements. But he is still not an arhat like me."

Then the Buddha thought, "No matter what wonders I perform, Kashyapa is not going to change his mind. I must try to shock him out of his rut." So just at the instant that Kashyapa was congratulating himself on being a great arhat, the Buddha said aloud, "Kashyapa, you are no arhat. Not only are you not an arhat, but following your present path you will never come even remotely close to becoming one."

This jolted Kashyapa all at once out of his blindness, and the ascetic fell on his face in front of the Tathagata and begged to enter homelessness under him and become a bhikshu. The Buddha told Kashyapa that he must consult his many followers also, since they were all bound up together. Kashyapa called the matted-hair ascetics together and explained the situation. They replied that for their part they had long had faith in the great monk, so if Kashyapa were going to enter homelessness under him, they would all certainly do so as well.

The next day, the river near the hermitage was clogged with matted hair and the fire-ritual utensils and other belongings of the ascetics. When they were all ready, the Buddha said to them, "Come, bhikshus. The Dharma has been properly proclaimed. Live the holy life for the complete ending of suffering." And thus they all became bhikshus, members of the Buddha's Sangha.

That day Kashyapa of the River and his three hundred ascetics, whose hermitage was downriver, saw the hair and all the rest floating in the current. They were afraid some disaster had befallen Kashyapa of Uruvilva and his community, so they went to find out. When they arrived, Kashyapa of Uruvilva told them of the conversion of himself and his community. Since Uruvilva Kashyapa was the elder and mentor of the three Kashyapas, after some talk, Kashyapa of the River and his followers also asked to join the Buddha. And the next day, Kashyapa of Gaya and his two hundred followers found their way into the Buddha's community as well.

5

Gathering the Sangha

IT WAS NOW APPROACHING seven years since the Buddha had left his palace and entered homelessness. And since he had passed out of the gates of Kapilavastu, Mara had been at his heels, searching for a weakness that might enable him to confuse and defeat the great being. He had still not given up. Now as the Buddha sat resting under a tree near the Nairanjana River, Mara came to him once more. "Here you sit brooding by yourself in the forest," he chided. "Are you sad because you are poor or have been driven away from home? Or is it because you have made no friends and are longing for company?"

"I am not sad at all," replied the Buddha. "Sadness has been drawn out of me by the root. I am free of all desires. There is nothing I long for, Thought-Twister."

"If there is a trace of ego left," Mara taunted, "that thinks 'I am the Enlightened One,' then, monk, I have you."

"Where I am, you cannot see; where I go, you cannot follow; what I teach, you cannot even perceive, Wrongdoer."

"If you have a path to follow that leads to the unborn beyond birth and death, by all means, take it! Go on alone! What need do you have to concern yourself with others?"

"Seekers ask me the way to the deathless realm. So I lead them where death ends, where nothing arises that could be reborn, to the end of suffering."

Mara was like a crab that had been fished out of a pool and deposited on dry land by children. Each time it stuck out a leg, the children would smash it with stones. Finally all its legs were gone, and it was unable to scuttle back to the pool. Such was now the case with Mara. All of his carping and mocking and twisting attempts to draw the Buddha into his thoughts had been disabled by the Blessed One, one after the other. Now he felt he could no longer even approach the great being.

"I am like the crow who walked around a stone that looked like a lump of fat, pecking for a soft bit here or a tasty morsel there. Like the crow, I must now go away disappointed." Letting his lute slip from his grasp, Mara slumped to the ground, dejected. After a while he picked up a stick and drew sixteen lines on the ground. With the first ten, he admitted to himself that the Blessed One had truly practiced the ten transcendental virtues and that, he, Mara, was no match for him in that. With the eleventh line, he recognized that, unlike the Buddha, he had no knowledge of the character and inclinations of all beings. For the twelfth, he acknowledged that he did not possess the Buddha's knowledge of beings' basic nature. For the remaining four, he confessed to himself that, unlike the Buddha, he had no tender compassion for all beings still caught in the miseries of existence, could not perform miracles, could not perceive everything existing, and could not attain perfect and supreme knowledge of the Dharma. In an odd way, Mara knew the Blessed One better than anyone else, and he had to confess his complete inferiority to the Great Bhikshu.

Mara's three daughters — Trishna (Craving), Arati (Ennui), and Raga (Lust) — came and found their father that way, abjectly scratching on the ground with a stick. When they had heard the tale of his woes, they hastened to console him. They told him they would soon find the Enlightened One's weak spot and bring him under Mara's power. Resignedly he told them that they would never prevail against the

Tathagata's indestructible mindfulness. They snickered and told him, "Don't worry. We know how to manage these matters."

Then they went to the Buddha and humbly pleaded to be allowed to remain with him so they could serve him and provide for all his needs and desires. The Buddha, sitting in meditative equipoise, did not so much as favor them with a glance. Thinking that their appearance might not correspond to his tastes, they adopted a variety of alluring guises, from heart-winning young girls and voluptuous dancers to fine middle-aged beauties. They plied the Blessed One with a variety of seductive or pathetic ploys and poses. Through all this he remained silent and unmoving. He did not even look at them. Finally he said, "I have attained the supreme wisdom, so nothing you can do can draw me back into the world of desire. Since in me the root of passion has been uprooted, how could you possibly ever succeed?" Having said that, he withdrew his attention from them again. Mara's daughters recognized that their efforts were futile. They stood before the Blessed One for a time, confused between frustration and awe. At last they could think of nothing more to do and returned to their father. Seeing them approach with a beaten look, he addressed them with these bitter words:

> *Fools! You have tried to split a rock*
> *By poking it with lily stems,*
> *To dig a hill out with your nails,*
> *To chew up iron with your teeth,*
> *To find footing on a cliff*
> *With a great stone upon your head,*
> *To push down a tree with your chest—*
> *And so you come from Gautama frustrated.*[12]

After staying at Uruvilva as long as he chose, the Tathagata went to Gayashirsha accompanied by a large following—the thousand bhikshus who shortly before had been matted-hair ascetics. In Gayashirsha there is a hill with a great rock on its slope, shaped like an elephant's head. The Blessed One with two or three attendants climbed to the top of this and uttered the following discourse:

"Bhikshus, everything is burning. The eye is burning, the nose is burning, the tongue is burning, the body is burning, the mind is burning. The consciousness of all these is burning. Visible forms, sounds, odors, flavors, touchable things, and mental objects are burning. Sense contact and mental contact is burning, and the feeling — pleasant, unpleasant, or indifferent — arising from sense and mental contact is burning. It is all burning with the fire of passion, the fire of aggression, and the fire of delusion. It is burning with birth, aging, and death. It is burning with sorrow, crying out, grief, pain, and despair.

"Seeing this, bhikshus, the noble disciple becomes dispassionate toward all this that is burning, toward the senses and the mind, their consciousness, their objects, their contact, and the feeling arising from these. Becoming dispassionate, his passion fades away. Thus his heart is liberated, and with that comes the knowledge that it has been liberated. He realizes that birth has been exhausted and the holy life has been lived to completion. What had to be done has been done. There is no more still to come."

When the Blessed One had uttered this discourse, all the thousand former matted-hair ascetics were entirely liberated from their defilements through absence of clinging. Thus all of them became arhats.

After this, the Blessed One with his thousand arhat disciples continued on toward the city of Rajagriha, traveling a part of the distance each day. At length, he stopped at a pleasant place outside the city where young palm trees had been planted around a large shrine.

Within the city, one of King Bimbisara's men told him, "The prince of the Shakyas who entered homelessness a few years ago has now arrived with a huge following of disciples. He is said to be fully enlightened, supreme in knowledge and action, omniscient, the teacher of gods and men. It is said he teaches a Dharma that is good in the beginning, good in the middle, and good in the end, both the words and the meaning, and he professes a holy life of pure conduct. Perhaps it would be good to go out and pay a visit to this lion of the Shakyas."

Then Bimbisara went out to meet the Blessed One outside the city, accompanied by a vast number of brahmin householders — in all, twelve hosts of one thousand householders each. Out of respect, the king dismounted from his chariot at a distance. He approached the Tathagata with palms joined, prostrated to him, touching his elaborate royal headdress to the ground, and then sat down off to one side. Of the thousands of householders, some prostrated and sat down, others went to greet the Buddha, doing so with varying degrees of deference, and still others merely sat down and waited. Gazing out over the crowd, the Buddha saw that many of the householders had noted the presence of Kashyapa of Uruvilva, who was seated near him, head shaven and wearing the saffron-colored robe of a bhikshu. He realized that since they were so used to regarding Kashyapa as the leader, they were wondering whether he was Kashyapa's disciple or it was the other way around.

The Blessed One then asked Kashyapa to explain what he had seen in the Buddha Dharma that had caused him to abandon the fire-ritual practice and join the Sangha. Kashyapa spoke up in a loud voice: "I have given up worshiping at the fires, because I saw that that worship was still fraught with worldly ambition. I saw that it does not liberate beings but leaves them enmeshed in the suffering of cyclic existence. Once I saw that, I no longer took pleasure in the powers I attained through this worship. Through the Buddha's Dharma, I realized a state of peace beyond the world of the senses in which there is no self and no other, no domination and no subjection, no possession and no loss."

Then he rose from his seat and approached the Blessed One. He prostrated to him and proclaimed, "The Sage of the Shakyas is my leader, my teacher, my guide. I am his fortunate disciple."

A murmur ran through the crowd. The Blessed One saw that Kashyapa's admission had opened the minds of the Magadhans, so he cleared his throat and began to speak. He gave his usual kind of progressive instruction, beginning with generosity and the abandonment of sense indulgence and proceeding gradually to the Four Noble Truths, dependent arising, and the nonexistence of self. After a while, understanding began to dawn in the Magadhans. By the time he had finished, a clear recognition of the Dharma arose in nearly all of them; that is, they nearly all directly realized that whatever is subject to arising is subject to cessation. The remainder of the householders, in whom such a vision had not arisen, were nonetheless convinced of the truth of the Buddha's words, and they too became his followers.

As for King Bimbisara, through listening to this discourse, he reached the independent knowledge of the Dharma that gives complete confidence, does away with all doubts, and frees one from external influences. Afterward, he said to the Blessed One, "Lord, when I was a boy I had five wishes: to be a king, to meet a fully enlightened arhat, to be able to show him respect, to be taught by him, and to understand his Dharma. Now all five of those wishes have been fulfilled." Then he invited the Buddha and the Sangha to accept their meal from him on the following day. The Buddha consented by remaining silent.

WHEN MORNING CAME, the Buddha took his bowl and outer robe and went into Rajagriha with his thousand bhikshus. Crowds of city folk looked on in wonder as they made their way through the streets to the king's palace. When they got there, the Buddha sat down on the seat that had been prepared for him, and King Bimbisara served him and the other bhikshus with his own hands, making sure that everyone was satisfied. When the Blessed One had finished eating and put down his bowl, the king sat down on one side. After a polite interval he announced to the Buddha that he wanted to make him a gift of a piece of land outside the city known as the Venuvana, or Bamboo Grove. He felt it had suitable qualities for a monastic retreat, because it was a lovely place and far enough away from the city so that the monks would not be disturbed by urban activity and noise, but close enough so that they could come for alms. Then the king rose and presented the gift in a formal ceremony, reciting a formula of donation while pouring water over the Buddha's hands from a golden pitcher.

The Buddha accepted the gift. Then he roused and delighted the king with words of Dharma, and when he was ready, he rose from his seat and departed.

At this time there were two young brahmins named Shariputra and Maudgalyayana living near Rajagriha with a community of wandering ascetics. These two had mastered the brahmanical texts at a very early age, and had wandered from home together in search of the deathless. One morning Shariputra observed a young bhikshu named Ashvajit gathering alms in Rajagriha. The young man had already gained mastery over his senses; thus he moved with grace and composure. His eyes were cast slightly downward, his gestures bespoke clarity and calm, and his attention did not wander. Shariputra was so touched by this evidence of spiritual attainment that he wanted to accost the young bhikshu on the spot in order to question him. But he felt it would be unsuitable to interrupt him on his alms round, so he followed him and waited for a more opportune moment. As Ashavajit was on his way back from the city, Shariputra finally addressed him. After a few words of greeting, he said, "From your serenity and radiance, I can plainly see that you have advanced far on the path of truth. Oh, tell me, have you found the deathless state? If so, please tell me, who is your teacher, or are you yourself a teacher?"

"The Enlightened One, Shakyamuni, is my teacher. Under him I have entered homelessness and been made a bhikshu," replied Ashvajit.

"Then please tell me, what is his teaching?" Shariputra responded, his eagerness unabated.

"I have but newly entered the order," said Ashvajit, "and can't really tell you much."

"Please be kind enough," said Shariputra, "just to give me the essence. Let us set aside the details for now."

So Ashvajit gave Shariputra this overall summary of the Buddha's teaching: "Of all things arising through a cause, the Tathagata has told the cause, and he has also shown their cessation. That is the teaching of the great monk."

Merely hearing these words was enough to make the pure vision of Dharma arise in Shariputra. He saw that all that arises also passes away. Up until this point he had been fixed on the idea of a permanent, uncaused self. This was a principal tenet of brahmanical doctrine. But when he heard Ashvajit's words, he suddenly realized that the sense of self, arisen from a cause, was also subject to cessation. This meant there was no obstacle to liberation.

Having experienced this clear vision on the spot, he went to tell his friend. Maudgalyayana saw Shariputra coming and immediately noticed that he was changed. "Shariputra, you are so radiant and alive," he said. "Tell me what has happened. Can it be that you've found the deathless state?"

"I have found it," said Shariputra. "I have really found it." And he told Maudgalyayana what had happened. Of course Maudgalyayana also wanted to hear the teaching the young mendicant had given his friend, so Shariputra repeated: "Of all things arising through a cause, the Tathagata has told the cause, and he has also shown their cessation. That is the teaching of the great monk."[13]

As soon as he heard these words, Maudgalyayana also experienced the same illumination. After a while he said to Shariputra, "We definitely must go to see Shakyamuni right away." And so they gathered their few things and set out to find him.

The Buddha saw Shariputra and Maudgalyayana coming in the distance. He said to the bhikshus around him, "That auspicious pair has already recognized the truth. Those two friends will be my chief disciples." There stood the two young men, still wearing matted hair and carrying the trident staffs of brahmanical wanderers. Now they approached the Buddha and prostrated to him. They declared their faith in his Dharma and requested to enter homelessness under him and join the order. The Blessed One had them shave their heads and don the saffron-colored robes. Then he said, "Come, bhikshus. The Dharma has been properly proclaimed. Live the holy life for the complete ending of suffering." And they became bhikshus.

Venerable Maudgalyayana became an arhat only a week later. But Shariputra spent two weeks keenly analyzing and reviewing the teaching on all levels of consciousness. Then he attained arhatship while staying with the Buddha at a cave near Vulture Peak Mountain in the vicinity of Rajagriha. He was standing behind the Buddha, fanning him and listening to a dialogue the Blessed One was having with a wandering ascetic named Dighanakha. Dighanakha was attempting to debate with the Tathagata, defending the thesis of repudiating all fixed views. The Buddha showed Dighanakha that this position brought him into conflict with holders of various views. Thus his position against views was itself a view that Dighanakha clung to in distinction to others. Then the Buddha spoke to him of truly relinquishing all conceptual viewpoints. As the Blessed One was explaining this with the power of direct knowledge, that same direct knowledge came over Shariputra, standing there behind him waving the fan. And Shariputra gained the independent realization of the Dharma that banishes all doubt.

In the years that followed, Shariputra became foremost in the Sangha in wisdom and insight, and Maudalyayana in the exercise of supernormal abilities.

WHILE THE BUDDHA was still staying near Vulture Peak Mountain, a brahmin from the Kashyapa clan, a young man of fine appearance and noble bearing named Pippali, appeared among the many seekers who daily came to hear the Buddha teach. He had given up his considerable wealth and a beautiful wife to wander in search of liberation. Now, from a fair distance back among the listeners, he saw the Blessed One for the first time, seated cross-legged, fully composed, radiating awareness and well-being, so that he seemed to the young brahmin to shine like pure gold. In the crush of people, there was not enough room for Pippali to prostrate, so he placed his palms together and bowed from the head and shoulders. Then, raising his voice as loud as he dared, he called out to the Buddha, "Please, lord, let me be your disciple."

The Buddha's eye picked out Pippali among the crowd. He saw that the young man had great longing for ultimate knowledge, that his mind was pure, and that he had already exerted himself considerably to find the truth. So the Buddha nodded at him and said, "Welcome."

This word of the Blessed One relieved Pippali of weariness and uncertainty, and opened his heart. He remained standing there, gazing at the Blessed One with rapt attention. The Buddha began speaking about the Dharma, but instead of giving progressive instruction as usual, he came to the essence of the teaching in only three or four sentences. Then, catching Pippali's eye, he held up a flower that lay by him, twirled it slightly in his hand, and smiled. At this gesture, the ultimate knowledge passed between the Buddha and Pippali. Outwardly, only a slight smile curved the young man's lips to indicate that he had understood. Afterward, because he had been able to attain the realization of an arhat with such sudden completeness, he was called Mahakashyapa, the Great Kashyapa. Years later, when the Buddha died, Mahakashyapa succeeded him as the leader of the Sangha.

It was also about this time that the Blessed One taught the Dharma to Naradatta, the nephew of the seer Asita, who had prophesied the Buddha's great destiny at the time of his birth. Naradatta heard the Buddha's teachings, meditated in solitude, and became an arhat. Later, under the name of Mahakatyayana, he was a powerful force in the spread of the Buddha Dharma.

IN KAPILAVASTU, KING Shuddhodana had been doing his best to keep informed of his son's doings. The king had heard he was teaching as an awakened one, a buddha, and had already gathered thousands of disciples, many of whom had become arhats. Shuddhodana was getting old. He felt he did not have many years remaining, and he wanted to see his son before he died. He sent as many as nine messengers with large retinues to request the Blessed One to visit Kapilavastu. Until now, no messenger had returned. Each, with his retinue, had fallen under the power of the Buddha's teaching. All these Shakyans had become bhikshus and remained with the Tathagata. Finally, the king hit upon the idea of sending the son of one of his ministers, Kalodayin, who had also been one of Siddhartha's childhood companions. The king felt that Kalodayin could be trusted to fulfill his mission no matter what he encountered. Also, he knew that the Buddha would recognize Kalodayin and perhaps be more likely to heed him than the others he had sent. Urgently he charged the young noble to do whatever was in his power to persuade the Buddha to come. Under no circumstances was he to fail to return with an answer.

Kalodayin arrived in winter at the Venuvana near Rajagriha where the Buddha was staying. He was astonished to find his childhood friend now surrounded by thousands of followers, with more homeless ascetics and householders pouring in every day to hear him teach. He felt himself and his mission belittled by the great scale of events at the Venuvana. He did not have the courage to come forward and deliver his message at once. He decided to wait a little in order to become more acquainted with the great matters in progress, thinking this would help him to act more effectively. Not long after his arrival, an opportunity arose to join the crowd listening to the Tathagata teach. He and his retainers were enthralled by the penetrating power of the Buddha's word, and as though impelled by an unstoppable force, they too soon became bhikshus. Some among them were quick to attain one or another of the four stages of realization culminating in arhatship. But when winter was over and the short, temperate period before the onset of summer had come, Kalodayin approached the Tathagata with the intention of persuading him to go to Kapilavastu. The Blessed One had long since recognized him and was quite willing to listen to his message.

After prostrating to the Buddha and exchanging polite inquiries with him, Kalodayin began extolling the beauty of the season, describing its virtues, and commenting on what a good time it was to travel. The Buddha expressed admiration for Kalodayin's poetic descriptions of the countryside, but did not delay in asking why he harped on the theme of traveling. "You seem to have some particular journey in mind," he said. Then Kalodayin told him how much his father loved him and dwelled upon him in his thought, and how much he longed to see him again before he died. And he spoke of the others in Kapilavastu as well. "Since, as it is already, the Tathagata is giving of himself so liberally to so many people, would it not also be right for him to consider his own kin and countrymen?"

It was now only five months since the first rainy season after his enlightenment spent at the Deer Park. The Tathagata had spent three months near Uruvilva, converting the three Kashyapas, and now two months in the neighborhood of Rajagriha. He decided that the time was ripe to respond to his father's request. So he replied favorably to Kalodayin and sent him ahead with the message.

Shortly thereafter, the Blessed One set out for the city he had left in the night nearly seven years ago. Traveling now with an enormous host of thousands of bhikshus, he covered only a few miles a day, and it took him nearly two months to reach Kapilavastu.

The Shakyans prepared a place for the Blessed One and his followers at the Nigrodha (Banyan) Park, close by Kapilavastu, where afterward a monastery would be built. When they heard he had arrived, the king and the nobles of the city came out to meet him, sending the children and younger people ahead with flowers. They themselves were decked out in their finery and wore flowers in their hair and garlands about their necks and bodies. They conducted the Blessed One to the park, where he sat down on the seat that had been prepared for him. The elders told the children and younger people to pay homage to the Buddha by prostrating. But those of high station who were older than the Blessed One felt that no such homage was in order. They regarded the Buddha as a younger brother, so they merely took their seats.

The Tathagata knew that with the solidity of the Shakyans' pride arrayed against him, it was not a fit situation for teaching. If they were lacking in veneration toward the teacher, their hearts would be closed

against the Dharma. To remedy the problem, the Blessed One performed various wonders. He even performed the twin miracle of making water and fire shoot forth from his body at the same time. This show
of wonders brought about the desired result. The king was deeply
moved. He stood and said, "When you were just born, witnessing the
seer Asita prostrate himself before you, I did the same. Later, when you
meditated beneath the tree at the plowing festival, and its shadow
remained still in order to protect you, I prostrated a second time. Now I
must make my third prostration." Shuddhodana joined his hands and
prostrated to the Buddha. Then the Shakyan nobles had no choice but
to relinquish their pride. They all rose and prostrated to the Blessed
One. After this an atmosphere of peace and well-being reigned over the
assembly.

Then a shower of rain began to fall out of a clear sky. This was
another wonder, for it rained on some of the Shakyans and not on
others. Then the Blessed One told them, "This is not the first time this
has happened in the assembly of my relatives." And he recounted the
tale of his previous life as Prince Vishvantara, during which a similar
event had occurred. The Shakyans were delighted with this tale. When
it was over, they all rose and left, but no one thought to invite the
Buddha and the Sangha for the following day's meal. The king did not
invite his son because he simply presumed the Tathagata would come
to his own house.

The next morning, when it was time for the alms round, the Blessed
One entered Kapilavastu. No one was there to take his bowl or invite
him to their house. So he reflected on whether the buddhas of the past,
when entering the city of their own kin, had simply gone begging from
house to house or had gone directly to the houses of their relatives.
Perceiving that they had begged from house to house, the Blessed One
began doing the same. The people looking from their windows were
stunned to see their prince, who was once borne about the city in a
golden palanquin, begging at the doors of ordinary people. Word of
these goings-on came also to Princess Yashodhara. She looked down

from her high window and saw her former husband moving through the street with the radiance and majesty of a buddha, yet begging. She ran to the king and told him, and the king himself hurried out into the street and confronted the Blessed One.

"Why do you shame us this way?" asked the king. "Did you think I would not provide for you and all your monks?"

"I am merely following our custom," said the Blessed One.

"This not our custom!" exclaimed the king. "From the time of our first royal ancestor in a remote age, not one of our royal lineage has begged in the street."

"It is not the custom of the royal lineage I am following, but rather of the lineage of buddhas. Countless buddhas of the past have begged from door to door, depending on the people for alms."

Having said this, the Blessed One went on speaking to his father about the buddhas and the holy life. He said there was little time to waste in adopting the holy life, for those who led it enjoyed bliss both in this life and in the next. As his father listened to the Tathagata speak, his mind was opened and he attained to the first of the four levels of realization. With some veils to his understanding removed, as the Blessed One went on speaking to him, he was able to perceive his meaning more directly. Thus a few minutes later in the same conversation, he attained to the second level as well.

Later on, King Shuddhodana would reach the third stage when the Buddha recounted to him the story of his own former life as Dharmapala. Later still, before dying, the king would attain arhatship. But now, as recognition of the truth of the Dharma dawned in him, he took the Blessed One's bowl and led him and his retinue to the palace. There he served them excellent food with his own hands. And when the Buddha had finished eating and put down his bowl, all the women of the household came before the Buddha and paid homage to him. At this time Queen Mahaprajapati, the Buddha's aunt who had raised him, also attained the first stage of realization.

But though she sent her maids and serving women to pay homage to the Buddha, Princess Yashodhara remained in her apartments, thinking to herself, "If the Blessed One values me, he will come to see me." So when the meal was finished, the Tathagata gave his bowl to his father to carry, and they went to Yashodhara's apartments. The Buddha entered and sat down on the seat that had been prepared for him. Yashodhara came at once to greet him. Grasping his ankles, she placed his feet on her head. Then King Shuddhodana told the Buddha about Yashodhara's loyalty to him. "When she heard that you wore saffron-colored robes, she too began to wear them. When she heard that you took only one meal a day, this became her custom too. When she heard that you no longer slept on a bed but on the ground, she also slept on a mat on the floor. When she heard that you had given up wearing flowers and perfume, she too gave that up. And when her relatives sent messages for her to return home, since they would gladly care for her, she merely ignored them. This is how loyal and good my daughter was," said the king.

"This is no wonder," said the Buddha. "It is not only in this life that she has shown loyalty to me in this way." And he told the story of his life as Chandrakinnara.

On the following day, the celebrations for the coronation, marriage, and house-blessing of Nanda, son of King Shuddhodana and Queen Mahaprajapati, were all to be celebrated. But now when the Buddha rose to leave, he handed his bowl to Nanda to carry, and since there was no point at which Nanda could bring himself to say to the Buddha, "Here is your bowl," he had no choice but to follow him out of the city to the Nigrodha Park. As they were leaving the palace, Nanda's bride-to-be, who was combing out her long, shining black hair at the window, caught sight of them and called out, "Don't be away long, my prince." When they reached the Buddha's sleeping place, the Buddha asked him if he would leave the householder's life and become a bhikshu. More out of awe than desire, the young man agreed. And the Blessed One ordained him.

Rahula, the Buddha's son, was now seven years old. One day soon after the Buddha's arrival in Kapilavastu, as the Blessed One was taking his meal at the palace, Yashodhara said to Rahula, "Do you see that monk there who is radiant like pure gold and who is the leader of all the others? That is your father. Now go to him, my son, and ask him for your inheritance." So when the Buddha had finished his meal, Rahula went to talk with him and said what his mother had told him to say. The Blessed One did not embrace the boy any more than he had any of his other relatives, nor did he show any other sign of particular affection. Nevertheless, Rahula told him, "It feels good even to stand in your shadow."

When the Buddha left the palace to return to the Nigrodha Park, the little boy followed just behind him, prattling about this and that and continuing to mention his inheritance. Since neither the palace folk nor the Buddha's attendants stopped him, and the Blessed One did not hinder him either, Rahula followed the Blessed One all the way to his sleeping place. When Rahula asked for his inheritance again, the Buddha had Shariputra enter him into homelessness, thus making him a novice monk.

After this, King Shuddhodana came to see the Tathagata. He prostrated to him and took a seat off to one side. After a few minutes of polite conversation, he said to the Buddha, "Please let me ask you a favor." The Blessed One replied that buddhas had done favors in the past if they were harmless and asked him what it was.

"Lord," replied the king, "I suffered no little pain when the Blessed One went forth. Then there was Nanda. Now Rahula is too much. Love for our children, Lord, cuts into the outer skin, then into the inner skin. Having cut into the inner skin, it cuts into the flesh and into the sinews. Having cut into the sinews, it cuts into the bones and reaches the marrow. There it remains. Lord, it would be good if the venerable ones did not receive children into homelessness without their parents' consent."

After that the Buddha roused his father's spirits by talking to him about the Dharma. Then he called the bhikshus together and made it a rule of the order not to receive a child into homelessness without the consent of his parents.

WHILE THE BUDDHA was at Kapilavastu, many of the Shakyan nobles were moved to renounce the householder life and enter homelessness under the Buddha. Many also attained one or another of the stages of realization, either immediately or later on. In addition, out of pride and loyalty, the Shakyans issued a decree that each family should provide one son to enter the Buddha's Sangha. Thus, either through desire or circumstances, a very large number of young Shakyans entered the order at this time.

However, when the Buddha left the country of the Shakyans to return to Rajagriha, there were many Shakyan princes still left who either wished to go or were obliged to do so. In one noble family, there were two brothers, Mahanama and Aniruddha, one of whom had to enter homelessness under the Buddha. Mahanama was the one who saw to the farming of the family lands and all the practical matters of their estate. Aniruddha was a sheltered youth who whiled away his time in idle pleasures. Aniruddha said he was too soft and delicate to face the homeless life, so Mahanama should go. Mahanama was willing, but pointed out that Aniruddha would then have to shoulder the household with all its practical labors. Aniruddha decided at once that he wanted to enter homelessness too. He asked his mother for permission so that he could go as well, but his mother opposed him. How could she agree to lose both her sons? But when Aniruddha pressed her again and again, she made a bargain with him. If his royal cousin Bhadrika, the young noble who had now taken over active rulership of the Shakyans, should agree to go as well, then so could Aniruddha. The mother thought she was safe. But Aniruddha finally prevailed on Bhadrika to give up his rulership and join the Sangha too.

So Mahanama, Aniruddha, and Bhadrika all set out to overtake the Buddha, who was traveling slowly through the country with an immense number of monks. When the Buddha's cousins Ananda and

Devadatta heard about this, they too decided to go, and they brought their friends Brighu and Kimbila. In addition, the young nobles brought their barber, Upali, along so he could cut their hair for them when the time came.

When they were far enough out of Shakya country not to be seen by anyone who knew them, the nobles had Upali cut their hair, and they also took off their rich ornaments and jewels and gave them to him to take back to Kapilavastu. "With this, you'll have enough to live on," they told him.

So Upali started on the homeward journey, carrying his bundle of riches. As he walked, however, he began thinking how things would go when he got home. "These noble Shakyans are fierce and proud," he thought. "They will be furious over the loss of their princes, and they certainly won't be happy about my ending up with their family valuables. They're certain to take it out on me somehow." And then, too, he realized that he was not a little disappointed at having to turn back without seeing the Blessed One. So he hung the bundle of riches on the branch of a tree and turned back to join the princes. When he caught up with them and explained himself, they agreed that he would have come to no good at the hands of their families. So they all went on their way together to find the Buddha.

It was in the mango grove at Anupiya in the country of the Mallans that they found the Blessed One. As soon as they could arrange an audience, they came to him, prostrated, and sat down off to one side. When the amenities were over, they requested the Blessed One to receive them into homelessness. "But," they said, "please receive Upali, our barber whom we have brought with us, into homelessness first. We are so full of pride about our noble birth, perhaps it would be good for us if for a while we had to show deference to Upali, to bow to him, stand up for him."

So the Buddha received Upali into the Sangha first and then the Shakyan princes. Later Upali was to become a major disciple of the Buddha, the principal authority on the Sangha's disciplinary rules.

In the course of the rainy season that followed, at Venuvana near Rajagriha, Bhadrika attained arhatship, Aniruddha attained the third level of realization, and Ananda the first. Devadatta acquired supernormal powers arising from powerful concentration, but failed to gain any realization of the truth.

DURING THIS PERIOD when Rahula was still a small child, the Buddha would occasionally spend time with him. He instructed him in ordinary things such as not lying and in developing judgment about what actions to cultivate and what actions to refrain from. Among other things, he taught him that telling lies was wasting the goodness in oneself. And he taught him to gauge actions by whether the fruits of them were beneficial or harmful.

The Buddha had to chastise his half-brother Nanda for going on his begging rounds wearing carefully pressed robes, painting his eyes, and using a glazed begging bowl. He also had to work with him time and again to keep him from leaving the Sangha on account of his sexual desire, and particularly his longing for the beautiful young woman he had been just about to marry. It is said that the Buddha diverted Nanda by taking him to one of the heavens, showing him five hundred incomparably beautiful celestial maidens, and telling him they would be his if he could master his mind. Later Nanda surrendered his attachment to sensuality and no longer had to be bargained with in this fashion.

6

Establishing the Dharma

THE BUDDHA SPENT the next two rainy seasons, the second and third after his enlightenment, at the Venuvana. When that third rainy season was over but the Blessed One had not yet begun his year's wanderings, a wealthy merchant from Rajagriha came to visit the community. Up to this time, the Buddha had never said anything about housing for the monks. They lived outdoors, under thick foliage where trees grew close together, in whatever habitable caves could be found, or under rocks — taking advantage of any natural shelter.

The merchant had great respect for the monks because they were mindful and controlled and carried themselves with modest grace. He felt bad seeing them living under rough conditions, so he went up to a group of them and asked them if they would live in shelters if he had them built. The monks replied, "The Tathagata has never said anything about permitting shelters."

"In that case, lords," said the merchant, "kindly ask the Tathagata about it and tell me what he says."

The monks brought the matter to the Buddha, and he gave his permission for the monks to live in shelters. The merchant immediately had a large number of huts and shelters built. Then he also invited the Buddha and the community to his house for the next day's meal. At the end of the meal, the merchant formally donated the shelters to the Sangha.

The merchant's brother-in-law was also a wealthy merchant. He came from Shravasti, the capital of the Koshalan kingdom to the north. His name was Sudatta, but he was generally called Anathapindada (Giver to the Defenseless) because of his great charity. On the day before the Buddha was to come, Anathapindada noticed that his brother-in-law was extremely busy giving orders to his servants about something, while he himself was being virtually ignored. He questioned his brother-in-law, who explained that the next day he was to be host to the Buddha and the Sangha.

When Anathapindada heard the word *Buddha*, he made his brother-in-law repeat it three times. That a buddha existed, a fully awakened one, and that he was nearby, became a fact so large in Anathapindada's mind that he could scarcely contain himself. He wanted to rush out to the Venuvana and see the Buddha immediately. But his brother-in-law convinced him that it was the wrong time to go and he should wait until the next day.

Anathapindada kept waking up during the night thinking it was already dawn. Well before daybreak, he ran out of patience. He stole quietly from the house and began making his way toward the Venuvana. It was a very dark night, and he did not know the way. Fright overtook him as he moved through the streets. When he came to the city walls, the gate opened and closed by itself. He found himself standing on the road, his skin crawling with terror. The fear was so great he could hardly take a step. He was tempted to run back to his brother-in-law's house but was not quite ready to give up. He remained standing just outside the gate, quaking with horror. A voice spoke in the darkness, saying, "A hundred elephants, a hundred horses, a hundred beautiful maidens laden with jewels are not worth so much as a tenth of one step forward at this very moment. Go forward, householder!" Finally Anathapindada overcame his fear and went on toward the Venuvana.

The Blessed One had gotten up before dawn and was pacing back and forth in front of his sleeping place. He saw Anathapindada coming and sat down in his seat to wait for him. When the merchant came near, the Buddha said, "Approach, Sudatta."

Anathapindada was thrilled that the Blessed One had called him by name. He prostrated at his feet and said that he hoped the Tathagata had slept well.

"Buddhas always sleep well," said the Buddha. "They are untouched by sensual desire, so their minds are cool. They have no sense of a solid self, so there is no conflict in their minds to disturb them. He who is at peace sleeps blissfully." Then he gave Anathapindada gradual instruction until the merchant reached the point of realizing that all that is subject to arising is subject to cessation. Then he instructed him further until independent knowledge of the Dharma was born in him. Anathapindada asked to be accepted as the Buddha's follower and was accepted.

Then he invited the Buddha and the Sangha for the following day's meal. The Blessed One indicated assent by remaining silent. When it was clear to Anathapindada that the Buddha had accepted, he rose, prostrated, and took his leave.

Anathapindada had everything prepared at his brother-in-law's house at his own expense, and the next day he served the Buddha and the community with his own hands. When the Buddha had finished eating and had put down his bowl, Anathapindada sat down at one side and asked, "Would the Buddha and the Sangha honor me by being my guests at Shravasti for the next rainy season?"

"Tathagatas take pleasure in secluded places where there is plenty of space," said the Blessed One. "If there were such a place, monks could easily come and go."

"Then, with your permission, I would like to build the Blessed One and the community a vihara, a monastery, in the neighborhood of Shravasti."

The Blessed One accepted this offer and directed Shariputra to accompany Anathapindada to Shravasti to supervise the building of the vihara. Then, having taught the Dharma to Anathapindada and others gathered at the merchant's house, he rose and departed.

Anathapindada set out for Shravasti, and all along the way he stopped and talked to people, telling them that a perfect buddha existed in the world and would be coming along that very road. He told them to prepare for him by planting gardens and setting up rest houses and readying gifts of food. This they did, and later on the Buddha and the Sangha benefited from the generosity of the people Anathapindada had spoken to all along their route.

Anathapindada looked all around Shravasti for a suitable site for the vihara, a place that was beautiful and secluded, yet close enough to the city so that bhikshus could gather alms and city people could come for teaching. Finally, he saw Prince Jeta's pleasure park, which he judged to be right in every way. He went to the prince and asked to buy the park. Intending to refuse him, the prince replied, "Only if you cover the entire park with gold pieces."

"Then the deal is concluded," said Anathapindada.

"There is no deal," said the prince, who was not inclined to part with the park at any price.

A legal dispute followed in which mediators concluded that once a price had been named and accepted, the transaction had become binding. So Anathapindada had gold pieces brought in carts and began covering the park with them. When the first cartloads were all used up, there was still a little area by the gate left uncovered. Anathapindada was just sending for more gold when Prince Jeta stopped him. The prince had been thinking that since Anathapindada was willing to put forth such a tremendous sum of money, it must be in service of something truly worthy. So he said, "Don't cover that space. That will be my gift."

Anathapindada thought, "It would be good if such an eminent person as the prince were associated with the Buddha's cause." So he let that spot at the entrance to the park be the prince's gift, and the prince had a fine gatehouse built on it.

Under Shariputra's direction, Anathapindada had buildings constructed in the park, which Anathapindada graciously called the Jetavana (Jeta's Grove). He had terraces and walkways laid out and leveled, rooms and halls built, storerooms and kitchens and baths built and fitted out, ponds dug, and outdoor pavilions constructed. All the needs of a large monastic community were provided for.

WHEN THE BLESSED One had remained as long as he chose in Rajagriha, he set out for Shravasti, traveling by slow stages. On the way, he stopped for a period of time near Vaishali in the country of the Videhans and stayed at the Kutagara (Peaked-Roof) Hall in the Mahavana (Great Grove). Since the Blessed One had given his permission for the Sangha to live in shelters, building work was going on everywhere, and here in the Mahavana as well. Problems arose in relation to the construction that had never existed in the community before, so the Blessed One had to lay down rules regulating supervision and allotment of work. And now that there were buildings and fixed accommodations of various kinds, disputes of an entirely new type came up regarding who was to have the use of the various desirable and less desirable spaces in the new buildings. So he also had to make rules regulating questions of this sort and establish an order of precedence within the Sangha.

When the Buddha finally arrived at Shravasti, he went to stay in the Jetavana. Anathapindada met him there and invited him and the community to the following day's meal, to which the Buddha assented in silence. When that meal was over and the Buddha had put down his bowl, Anathapindada sat down to one side and asked the Buddha what the proper way to present the vihara was. The Buddha told him to present it to "the Sangha of bhikshus of the four directions and of the past, present, and future." So the merchant rose and, using this formula, which afterward became the customary one, formally presented the Jetavana Vihara while pouring water over the Buddha's hands from a golden pitcher.

Then the Awakened One gave his blessings on this great occasion, praised the usefulness of viharas and the act of donating them to the community. The dedication festival for the great vihara lasted nine months.

Another great monastery was built for the Buddha's community by King Prasenajit, who reigned over the Koshalans in the capital city of Shravasti. The king was at first skeptical about the Buddha. He especially wondered how the great leader dared to call himself a buddha, when none of the other eminent spiritual teachers of the day thought of doing so. But Prasenajit's wife, Queen Mallika, who was a very able and intelligent woman, often spoke to the king in favor of the Blessed One, and finally convinced Prasenajit to see him in person. After the first time Prasenajit heard the Buddha teach, he asked to be accepted as his follower. As time went on, the king became more and more devoted to the Tathagata. He eventually built a great vihara known as the Rajakarama, in the vicinity of Shravasti. The Buddha pronounced a number of well-known discourses in King Prasenajit's presence.

BY THIS TIME, the Buddha's community numbered many thousands of bhikshus, and occasionally complaints came to his ears about harm done to vegetation and wildlife as a result of their wandering over the countryside throughout the year. The bhikshus were already held to rules of strict simplicity, making their demand on the world around them as small as possible. Now the Blessed One made it obligatory for bhikshus to remain in a vihara or other retreat place throughout each rainy season. Thus, for a considerable part of each year, they were able to concentrate on their meditative discipline and remain largely out of the way of the lay population.

The rainy season that the Buddha spent at the Jetavana at Anathapindada's invitation was the fourth after his enlightenment. The fifth rainy season he stayed in the Kutagara Hall in the Mahavana near Vaishali. Not long after this, his father, Shuddhodana, became seriously ill, and the Tathagata went once more to Kapilavastu. When he arrived there, his father was on his deathbed. During his father's last days, the Blessed One was frequently at his bedside. He soothed the king's pain and talked to him a great deal about the Dharma. The understanding between them was so tender and direct that before the king died he was able to gain the realization of an arhat.

Around this time, there was a dispute between the Shakyans and the neighboring Kolyans about the use of the water in the Rohita River, which formed the border between their two realms. The water was low, and there was not enough of it to irrigate on both sides. The dispute had led them to the brink of war. The rival armies were arrayed against each other on opposite sides of the little river when the Buddha arrived with the intention of averting bloodshed. A seat was prepared for him, and he sat down with the opposing leaders. First he asked what the matter of contention was, but the princes and generals had no idea what the root problem was. They only knew there had been challenges and insults on both sides, and attacking with armed force had become a matter of honor. Down the chain of command the Buddha's question went without encountering anyone who knew the answer. It finally took the local farmers to explain that it was a matter of water for irrigation. The Buddha then asked the leaders what the value of a little water was. Not so great, they thought. And what was the value of a little earth? Again not so great. "But what about the value of the blood of princes?" he asked them. That they thought was very precious. "So you are about to destroy what is extremely precious for the sake of something of little value?"

Talking in this way, the Buddha gradually pacified the anger on both sides. Then, by telling them various tales from his previous lives, the Blessed One helped the opposing parties to see matters in a larger perspective. Finally they settled their dispute and made peace.

Then the Shakyans and Kolyans, acknowledging that the Buddha had saved many hundreds of lives on both sides, decided to dedicate two hundred and fifty men each to the Sangha to become monks. Thus the grief of wives at parting forever from their husbands was not entirely spared by averting battle.

MEANWHILE, QUEEN MAHAPRAJAPATI Gautami had conceived the desire to devote herself to the spiritual life. Her husband was dead, and both her son Nanda and Rahula, who was like a grandchild to her, had entered homelessness under the Buddha. Now she too wanted to become a member of the Blessed One's Sangha. But there was no such thing as a female member, a bhikshuni, a nun, of the community of the Buddha. While the Buddha was still at Kapilavastu, she came to him, accompanied by many of the wives of the five hundred soldiers who had been compelled to enter the Sangha after the confrontation at the Rohita. She prostrated and stood to one side, and said, "Lord, it would be good if women too could enter homelessness under the Tathagata and follow the discipline prescribed for the holy life."

"Enough, Gautami," said the Buddha. "Do not ask this."

The queen repeated her request a second and a third time and received the same answer. There was nothing more she could say, so she prostrated and went away, disappointed and unhappy.

When the Blessed One had stayed in Kapilavastu as long as he chose, he set off for Vaishali. After some days on the way, he arrived and took up residence in the Kutagara Hall.

In the meantime Mahaprajapati, thinking that if the women showed courage and determination, the Buddha would not be able to refuse them, decided to gather them together and follow the Buddha to Vaishali. The women had their hair cut, put on saffron-colored robes, took alms bowls, and set off on foot. Many of them were noblewomen who had hardly gone beyond the courtyards of their houses without being carried in litters. They had always been pampered by servants and had soft hands and feet. Now, day by day, they plodded along dusty roads toward Vaishali, begging their food as they went. When they arrived at the Mahavana, Mahaprajapati went to the Kutagara Hall and stood waiting outside, hoping for an opportunity to see the Blessed One.

Her feet were sore and swollen, she was covered with dust, and she was nearly sobbing with exhaustion.

Ananda found her and asked how she came to be standing there that way. He was filled with pity and sympathy at the sight of her. She explained that she and the others had come to ask the Tathagata once again to be admitted to the Sangha. Ananda told her to wait, and went inside the house where the Buddha was staying to speak to him. He told him of Mahaprajapati standing outside and said, "It would be good if women could leave the householder's life and enter homelessness as part of the order."

The Buddha said, "Enough, Ananda. Do not ask that women be allowed to enter the order."

Twice more Ananda asked and received no better answer. This was equivalent to a refusal, and Ananda should have given up and retired. But instead he thought of asking the Buddha in another way. So he said, "If women did renounce the householder's life and enter homelessness, would they be capable of attaining the four levels of realization?"

"They would," replied the Buddha.

"That being the case," continued Ananda, "since Mahaprajapati nursed and raised the Tathagata like her own son when his own mother died and was benefactor to him in so many ways, and now has come all this way on foot, is standing outside with feet swollen and bleeding, could you not consider allowing women to enter homelessness as members of the Sangha?"

In the face of this plea, the Buddha relented. He said he would accept Mahaprajapati into the Sangha if she would accept eight special conditions. If she merely agreed to the conditions, that would count as full ordination for her. And he enumerated eight points having to do with bhikshunis' deferring to and depending upon the authority of bhikshus in a variety of circumstances. Then Ananda went outside and told Mahaprajapati the eight conditions. She accepted them unhesitatingly and with great joy. Thus she became the first bhikshuni.

Ananda went back inside the Hall to report the matter done. Then

the Buddha told him, "If women had not been permitted to enter the
Buddha's Sangha, the holy life as established by him would have lasted
a very long time, a thousand years. Since women have now been
admitted, it will only last five hundred years. In an effort to keep matters
from becoming still worse, I have established these eight special rules,
which should never be transgressed under any circumstances." Then
he told him that bhikshus could ordain the other women as bhikshunis
following the usual procedure.

Mahaprajapati availed herself of every opportunity to receive instruction from the Tathagata. She practiced meditation intensively in seclusion, and after not too long a time was able to attain arhatship. Many of
the other women who were ordained at this time soon began to attain
the various stages of realization.

The Tathagata's former wife, Yashodara, also eventually enterered
the order, and she too was able to attain arhatship. She was particularly
gifted in supernormal powers and became foremost among the
bhikshunis in that manifestation of awakened mind.

After having passed the sixth rainy season in the neighborhood of
Shravasti, the Blessed One returned to Rajagriha. It was then that he
converted another one of his leading disciples. King Bimbisara had an
extraordinarily beautiful wife whose name was Khema. Khema always
avoided the Buddha because she had heard that he placed a low value
on physical beauty. However, one day she was on a pleasure outing to a
garden near the Venuvana where he was teaching. She saw the crowds
and was drawn by curiosity just to catch a glimpse of him. Knowing she
was there, the Buddha created the image of an exquisitely beautiful
heavenly maiden standing behind him and fanning him as he spoke.
Queen Khema was captivated by the phantasmic maiden and remained to admire her beauty. As she watched the maiden gracefully
fanning the Blessed One, he made the beautiful image change from
youth to middle age and then to old age. The maiden's skin gradually
became wrinkled and her hair gray; her teeth fell out, and flesh hung
from her body shapelessly. Finally, when the image had become com-

pletely decrepit, it collapsed to the ground. Seeing this, Khema realized the truth of the Dharma, that all that is subject to arising is subject to cessation. Soon after, with the king's permission, she entered the Sangha. In the course of time, she too became an arhat. The Buddha made her head of the Sangha of bhikshunis along with another female arhat, Utpalavarna. Khema was considered foremost in wisdom and insight among all the bhikshunis.

DURING THIS PERIOD of the Buddha's teaching, as the Sangha grew in numbers and became widespread throughout the valley of the Ganges and its tributaries, it came into competition for the favor of kings and householders with six other major orders of wandering mendicants, among them the Jains, led by their founder, Nirgrantha Jnaniputra (called Mahavira), and the Ajivikas, led by Maskarin Goshaliputra. The leaders of all the orders claimed to be spiritually realized and to teach the real truth, and there were often debates or other kinds of confrontations between the members of these mendicant orders in which the lay population took sides.

A rich merchant in Rajagriha had a beautiful begging bowl made of the finest sandalwood and attached it to the top of a very tall pole in the square in front of his shop. He let it be known that any mendicant, no matter what order he belonged to, who possessed the power to levitate and take the superb bowl down could keep it. A number of attempts had been made to get the bowl either by supernormal power or by persuading the merchant that the suitable recipient had arrived. A number of monks of the Buddha's order, with Maudgalyayana at the head, passed by the spot one day. There was a crowd present, and the monks thought it would redound to the glory of the Sangha if one of their number were to levitate and take the bowl. Maudgalyayana, for whom this would have been a trifling manifestation of power, declined to make a show of his abilities. But one of the other monks, Pindola-Bharadvaja, rose in the air and remained there for a long time so that he could be seen by everybody. Then he took the bowl and came down.

When the Buddha heard of this, he chastised the monks, saying that such displays would not in the long run bring people to see the truth of the Dharma. He made it a rule that Sangha members should not exhibit their supernormal powers.

But then matters came to a head in Shravasti in a major confrontation between the Buddha and the leaders of the other sects. With royalty and nobles and large numbers of the general populace in attendance, the Buddha defeated the others in debate. Then, when some of the other teachers began to show miracles, the Buddha once again performed the twin miracle of emanating fire and water from his body at the same time. Then he caused an immense jeweled platform to appear in the air and taught the Dharma to the crowd while pacing back and forth upon it.

After his resounding defeat of the rival teachers, the Buddha rose to the Heaven of the Thirty-three to teach the Dharma to his mother, who had been reborn as a goddess. He spent the seventh rainy season after his enlightenment in that heaven teaching her and the other deities the Dharma. As a result of this time spent with her, the goddess who had been the Buddha's mother was able to attain arhatship.

AFTER THE SEVENTH rainy season, the Buddha returned to the Jetavana near Shravasti. He was now more than ever revered and esteemed by the people there. Food, cloth for robes, and medicine were provided in plenty for the Sangha, but members of the other mendicant communities did not have such an easy time. Direct confrontation with the Tathagata had proved fruitless. Now attempts were made to discredit the Buddha in another way.

An ascetic by the name of Chincha was induced to begin visiting the Jetavana Vihara and to make sure that her frequent visits were noticed. After a suitable period of time, she returned to the Jetavana one day with her body rounded and full like a woman at the end of pregnancy. In front of a crowd of people, she demanded that the Buddha provide her with a place to give birth, since he was the one responsible for her condition. "Only you and I know if what you are saying is true," said the Buddha. And just then the fastenings of her dress gave way, and the pillows with which she was shamming pregnancy were revealed to everyone.

Quite some time later, conspirators against the Buddha got an ascetic by the name of Sundari to make frequent visits to the Jetavana and make sure that she was seen. After a period of time they killed her and buried her on the Jetavana grounds. Then they reported her missing to the authorities and helped them find the corpse. It appeared as though she had been murdered by the monks.

A scandal arose in which the monks were accused of violating the woman and then killing her to hide their misdeeds. Begging monks were reviled in the streets for pretending to be holy while committing heinous crimes. The bhikshus were horrified and came to the Buddha to ask him what to do. He told them when they were insulted not to be provoked. Remaining unruffled, they should merely repeat a little doggerel he gave them, which said that liars and murderers eventually suffer the fruits of their actions. He told them the scandal would pass in seven days. Seeing the bhikshus behaving serenely, the people began to think they really had not committed the crime. And by the time seven days had passed, the people stopped maligning them, and the trouble died away.

THE BUDDHA PASSED the eighth rainy season in the country of the Bhargas near Mount Sumsumara. Sometime after the retreat was over, he went into the town of Sumsumaragiri for alms. He encountered a householder and his wife who were called Father Nakula and Mother Nakula. As soon as they saw him, they fell at his feet and said, "O son, where have you been so long?" The Tathagata saw that Father Nakula had been his father, grandfather, and maternal uncle in the course of hundreds of previous lives, and Mother Nakula had been his mother, aunt, and grandmother. The Buddha gave no ostensible sign, only instructed them extensively in the Dharma until they both reached the first stage of realization in which they saw that all that is subject to arising is subject to cessation. Later on, he visited them again and received a meal from them. On that occasion, they declared that through countless existences they and their son had been lovingly together and had never so much as said an insulting word to one another. They expressed their wish to continue that way in the present and future lives. The Buddha received their words warmly, and afterward spoke kindly of them both to his bhikshus and other people.

The Buddha continued wandering through this country for some months, encountering both wealthy and ordinary people, and setting many people's feet on the path of Dharma. Then, invited by some wealthy merchants, he spent the ninth rainy season near Kaushambi on the Yamuna River in the country of the Vatsans. There were already four large viharas in this region.

It was after this rainy-season retreat that a petty quarrel arose between two bhikshus in one of the viharas near Kaushambi that grew out of proportion and threatened the unity of the Sangha. One of the bhikshus was a specialist in monastic discipline, which is called vinaya. He was occupied with committing to memory and interpreting the rules made by the Buddha for the behavior of the Sangha in all circumstances of monastic life, and he taught this knowledge to his students. The other bhikshu was a specialist in the Buddha's doctrinal discourses, called sutras. His work was to memorize the sutras and develop an orderly knowledge of their content, and he too passed on his knowledge to his students.

One day the sutra specialist left a bowl containing some unused washing water in the privy. This was found by the vinaya specialist, who had gone there after him. The vinaya specialist asked the sutra specialist if he knew he had left the bowl of water there, and the sutra specialist said he did. The vinaya specialist then asked him if he knew that that was an infringement of the rules. He said he did not. The vinaya specialist told him it was, and the sutra specialist said that he would acknowledge that infringement. "But," the vinaya specialist told him, "if you did it without intention out of lack of awareness, then it is not an infringement." And the sutra specialist went away, thinking the matter was settled and that no infringement had been committed by him.

The vinaya specialist began telling others that the sutra specialist had committed an infringement. He was asked to acknowledge his infringement. Now he refused to do so and said that the vinaya specialist had behaved with deceit. The vinaya specialist convoked an assembly in which the sutra specialist was suspended from the order for failing to acknowledge an infringement. The sutra specialist, who was a learned and influential teacher, refused to accept the suspension. He gathered many supporters, and so did the vinaya specialist. The two parties continued to squabble, and tension and dissension grew.

Some bhikshus who were troubled brought the matter to the Tathagata. The Tathagata said, "There is going to be a schism in the Sangha." Then he went to see the bhikshus who had ordered the suspension, and urged them to be temperate and recognize that it was unnecessary to suspend a learned and well-intended bhikshu for an infringement that he did not see as one—particularly when the result was a painful disunity in the Sangha.

Then he went to the party of the suspended bhikshu and told them that it was wrong to fail to acknowledge an infringement simply because one does not see it as infringement. One should acknowledge it anyway out of faith in those who think it is an infringement—particularly when the result of not doing so was a painful disunity in the Sangha.

But neither side heeded the Blessed One, and the wrangling and quarreling and venomous slandering got worse and worse. A monk came to the Blessed One and recounted this to him. He begged him once more to speak to the contending parties. The Buddha did so and asked them to put an end to the discord. The reply of the two parties was that the Blessed One should stay out of the matter, since all the ugliness of it would never be blamed on him anyhow. The Buddha repeated his request twice more, and twice more got the same answer. Then he got up and went away.

The following morning the Blessed One went into Kaushambi for alms. When he got back, he set his sleeping place in order and picked up his bowl and outer robe. While standing, he began to speak. He spoke about the ludicrous blindness of those embroiled in quarrels, how they always see fault and blame elsewhere. Even thieves and murderers can agree among themselves, he said, but not these warring bhikshus. He ended with these words:

> If you can find a trustworthy companion
> With whom to walk, both virtuous and steadfast,
> Then walk with him content and mindfully. . . .
> If you can find no trustworthy companion . . .
> Then as a king who leaves a vanquished kingdom,
> Walk like a tusker [bull elephant] in the woods alone.
> Better it is to walk alone:
> There is no fellowship with fools.
> Walk alone, harm none, and know no conflict;
> Be like a tusker in the woods alone.¹⁴

Having said these words, he departed.

The Blessed One walked to a village near which the bhikshu Brighu was living by himself. This was one of the Shakyan princes who had come to the Buddha long ago with the barber Upali. He sat and talked with Brighu about small things for a while, then instructed him in the Dharma. When he was satisfied, he got up and resumed walking. He went on until he came to the Eastern Venuvana, where Aniruddha and Kimbila and another monk, named Nandya, were staying together. When he reached the boundary of the park, the Tathagata was stopped by a man guarding the park who told him he could not enter because there were some bhikshus in retreat there. Aniruddha, however, heard the conversation and came out and told the man, "This is our teacher, the Buddha himself. Don't keep him out of the park."

Then all three monks came out to meet the Blessed One, and he inquired about their welfare and whether they were able to live together in harmony and kindness without getting into quarrels. Aniruddha told him that the three of them got on together very well. He told him he felt fortunate to be living the holy life with such companions and thought well and kindly about them both in public and private. He felt so kindly toward them that he was always willing to give in to how they wanted to do things. And he thought it was the same from their side as well. "We are different in body, but one in mind, I think." He went on to describe how they cooperated closely, helping one another in all the details of their simple existence. He finished by saying that they lived for the most part in silence, but every fifth night they sat up all night discussing the Dharma.

The Blessed One inspired them further by instructing them in the Dharma. Then he got up and continued on his way.

He wandered for some days until he came to the Parileyyaka forest. He went into the thick jungle and stayed for a time in solitary retreat. One day he thought, "Not so long ago I was living in discomfort, tormented by the endless squabbling of those Kaushambi monks who were stirring up strife in the community. Now, alone, I am so very comfortable and at ease without all of them."

At the same time there was in the forest a bull elephant who had been tormented by the carryings-on of all the cow and calf elephants of the herd, having to eat trampled food and drink water dirtied by other elephants, being bumped and shoved by the cow elephants at bathing time. He, too, thought, "Why should I not live alone and get away from all this trouble?" So he too went off to the Parileyyaka forest and into the thick part of the jungle, and found the Blessed One meditating there at the foot of a shala tree. The elephant looked after the Buddha by bringing him food and water and clearing away the thick undergrowth in front of his meditation place so that he could pace back and forth. The elephant thought, "I used to be tormented by the herd, but now, alone, I am so content."

Knowing the elephant's mind, the Blessed One said these words:

Tusker agrees with tusker here;
The elephant with tusks as long as [cart] shafts
delights alone in the woods:
Their hearts are thus in harmony.[15]

In Kaushambi it was not long before the monks discovered that the Blessed One had put his place in order and disappeared. They became upset and started talking about how terrible it was that the Buddha had gone off by himself without informing anybody. They thought some monks should go after him and find out where he was. But Ananda told them, "When the Blessed One sets his place in order and goes off by himself without telling anyone, it means he wants to live alone. Nobody should follow him."

After some time had passed, a group of monks came to Ananda and said how much they would like to hear a discourse on the Dharma from the Blessed One himself again. So Ananda set off with this party of bhikshus, and they eventually found the Blessed One meditating under the shala tree. They prostrated to him and sat down off to one side. The Blessed One then gave them instruction in the Dharma.

The Buddha spent the tenth rainy season after his enlightenment in the Parileyyaka forest. After he had been there as long as he chose, he set off for Shravasti, traveling in slow stages. At Kaushambi, the lay people began to see the bhikshus there as no more than troublemakers who had driven the Blessed One away so that they could no longer get to see him. They stopped showing the bhikshus deference, and what was worse, they refused to supply them with food. Finding themselves rejected and without support, the contending factions of bhikshus finally decided to go to the Jetavana where the Buddha was and settle their dispute in his presence.

Many of the Tathagata's chief disciples were with him at the Jetavana when the word came that the Kaushambi bhikshus were on their way. To these disciples, dealing with those bhikshus was like handling a bundle of stinging nettles. Each disciple came separately to confer with the Buddha about how to receive the bhikshus, how to speak with them, how to house them, how to feed them — everything seemed like a problem. The Blessed One gave instruction to each disciple in a manner corresponding to his or her character and understanding, but in essence told them all to deal with the Kaushambi bhikshus even-handedly in accordance with the Dharma.

Eventually, after much to-do, the sutra specialist who had been suspended acknowledged having committed an infringement. This made it technically possible for the party of the vinaya specialist to reinstate him as a member of the community, and they did so. Thus the dispute was settled, and the procedural precedent for settling such disputes was noted.

THE ELEVENTH RAINY season was spent in the vicinity of Rajagriha. Following it the Buddha began wandering through the country of the Magadhans. One morning, near the village of Ekanala, he was at the large farmstead of a brahmin farmer named Bharadvaja at the time of day when the latter was providing food for his laborers. The Buddha stood among the men with his alms bowl and silently waited to receive some food. When he came to the Buddha, Bharadvaja said, "I plow and sow, and when I have done that, then I eat." The Buddha replied that he too plowed and sowed, and having done so, also ate. Bharadvaja said, "Master Gautama, I don't see your plow, I don't see your plowshare, I don't see your goad, I don't see your oxen."

The Buddha responded, "In my work, faith is the seed, control is the rain, the yoke and plow are understanding, modesty is the plow shaft, mind is what ties the yoke on, and mindfulness is both the goad and the plowshare blade. With body and speech controlled, and eating sparely, I reap with the hoe of truth. My ox is energy which pulls on toward liberation. Going beyond sorrow and never turning back is the plowing I do. What I reap is the unborn, the deathless. Whoever does likewise will be freed of all suffering."

Bharadvaja stood there in the hot sun and listened to these words along with his gathered laborers. He was moved by them and immediately went to fetch the Buddha some milk-boiled rice, which he gave to him in a large bronze vessel. However, the Tathagata refused the rice, saying he did not take food for singing a song. "Moreover," he said, "the rice is not fit to eat. Throw it away in some flowing water." When the brahmin threw the rice into the water, it steamed and fumed as though it had acid in it. When Bharadvaja saw that, he knew that the Buddha had clear sight, and he realized that his teaching must be true. He prostrated at the Blessed One's feet and took the threefold refuge.

BY THIS TIME the Blessed One's son, Rahula, was eighteen. As always, he stayed near his father whenever he could. He followed him on the alms round and tried to be present whenever he was teaching. And the Blessed One progressed in his instruction to the lad from basic character-building to advanced instruction in meditation and seeing through the sense of self. Now the Blessed One and Shariputra were giving him meditation instruction, both from the angle of insight and from that of mindfulness of breathing. The Blessed One taught him to meditate on not identifying any of the five skandhas (form, feeling, perception, conceptual formations, and consciousness) with a sense of self. Then he taught him how to meditate on not identifying any of the five elements (earth, water, fire, air, and space) as they are found in one's individual makeup with a sense of self. Then he gave him further instruction on how to let his mental development take on the virtues of each of the five elements, since each one has a different quality of equanimity inherent in it. At one point he told him: "Practice lovingkindness to get rid of ill will. Practice compassion to get rid of cruelty. Practice sympathy to get rid of apathy. Practice onlooking equanimity to get rid of resentment. Practice contemplation of loathsomeness in the body to get rid of lust. Practice contemplation of impermanence to get rid of the conceit 'I am.' Practice mindfulness of breathing; for when that is maintained and developed, it brings great fruit and many blessings."[16] The Buddha also taught Rahula thirty-two different ways to practice mindfulness of breathing. The young man was usually eager for instruction, and he meditated diligently in order to gain direct knowledge of what had been taught him.

Later that year, the Tathagata was staying at Veranja when the brahmin named Veranja came to see him. He had heard that the Buddha did not stand up to greet brahmins, even aged ones, or offer them a seat. He reproved the Buddha for this. The Blessed One told him that he did not know of a being in the entire world system to whom he should show such deference. If the Tathagata were to do that for anyone, he explained, it would be such a controversion of the right order of things that that person's head would split in pieces.

The brahmin then asked a series of questions aimed at reducing the Buddha's position to absurdity by logic. The Buddha replied to the brahmin's logical points but spun his answers into a Dharma discourse so inspiring that it led to Veranja's conversion on the spot. The brahmin not only took the triple refuge but also invited the Buddha and the Sangha to be his guests for the next rainy season, an offer which the Buddha accepted. Thus the twelfth rainy season was spent at Veranja.

THERE WAS A famine at this time in this region, and alms food was not available from householders. The only food the bhikshus could get was bran meant for horse fodder, which was donated by horse traders. When the first bran was given, Ananda took a portion of it and ground it in a mortar for the Blessed One in order to make it finer and easier to digest. Now, it is said of the buddhas that they may know of something and ask about it or know of it and not ask. They only ask about something when some good will come of asking. They only ask in order to teach or to make known a training precept. Often they let matters pass by in silence. In this case the Buddha asked Ananda what the sound of the mortar was. Ananda told him the only food they could get was horse fodder, and he had been grinding it finer for the Blessed One. The Blessed One declared that it was wonderful that the monks could make do with such fare, and he lamented that future generations would look down on much better food.

Then Maudgalyayana said that there was food rich like honey under the earth's surface at a certain depth. He offered to turn a portion of the earth over by means of his supernormal powers in order to procure food for the Sangha. The Buddha told him that it would not be good to upset the natural order in this way for their food. "Beings will be upset," he explained.

During this period Shariputra asked the Buddha in the case of which past buddhas had the holy life they had propounded lasted for a particularly long time. The Buddha told him, naming the past buddhas. Shariputra then asked the Blessed One why the dispensations of certain other buddhas had lasted only a short time. "Those tathagatas were not forthcoming in teaching the Dharma in detail. They did not give great numbers of discourses in which all aspects of doctrine were elaborated explicitly, nor answer a great number of questions and have the answers duly noted and memorized, nor recount many tales of their previous lives. And they did not declare the pratimoksha, the code of behavior, for the Sangha. Thus, when those disciple who became enlightened through direct personal contact with the tathagata died away, there were no threads to hold the holy life of the community together. Those tathagatas just read their disciples' minds and gave them suitable advice."

The Blessed One went on to tell this story: "Once, in a jungle thicket, the Blessed One Vishvabhu, accomplished and fully enlightened, read the minds of a community of bhikshus a thousand strong, and this was how he advised and instructed them: 'Think thus; do not think thus. Give attention thus; do not give attention thus. Abandon this; enter upon and abide in this.' Then, through following his instructions, their hearts were freed from defilements through not clinging. And that jungle thicket was one so awe-inspiring that normally it would make a man's hair stand on end if he were not free from emotion. That was the reason why those Blessed Ones' holy life did not last long."[17]

Having heard this, Shariputra stood up and placed his palms together and formally requested the Buddha to proclaim the pratimoksha, the monastic code of behavior, then and there so that the holy life he taught would last a long time. The Buddha told him to wait until he himself should see that the time was ripe. "The pratimoksha should only be made known in response to the arising of certain untoward manifestations in the Sangha. Some of those unwholesome manifestations will not come about until the community has become larger and more developed in a variety of ways."

Then the Blessed One indicated that it was proper to formally take leave of their host for the rainy season before carrying on. So they went to see Veranja, who invited them for a meal. When the meal was done and the Buddha had put down his bowl, Veranja apologized for not providing everything for the monks as he should have. Then he presented the Sangha with two pieces of cloth for robes for each monk. Then the Blessed One instructed Veranja in the Dharma, and when he had finished, he got up and went away.

The Buddha passed the thirteenth rainy season at a place called Chalika. In the year following that, Rahula reached the age of twenty and was therefore old enough for full ordination. On the occasion of this ceremony, the Tathagata instructed his son at length and in detail on impermanence, non-ego, and the giving up of attachments. In the course of this talk, through nonclinging, Rahula's mind was entirely liberated from defilements. Thus he reached arhatship and full monkhood on the same day.

The fourteenth rainy season was spent at the Jetavana near Shravasti, and the fifteenth at Kapilavastu. While the Blessed One was at Kapilavastu he had to face the rancor of Yashodhara's father, Suprabuddha, who had never forgiven the Buddha for abandoning his daughter. The old man got drunk one day and blocked the Buddha's way on the street as the Blessed One was going about his alms round. He lay on the ground across the Buddha's path and lashed him with coarse insults one after the other. The Blessed One looked on with equanimity for a time, then turned to Ananda and predicted that as a result of treating a tathagata in this fashion, Suprabuddha would soon meet a dire end.

Then he turned and continued his alms round in another direction. Seven days later the earth opened and swallowed the embittered noble at the doors of his palace.

The sixteenth rainy season was spent in Alavi. There the Buddha is said to have quelled a child-eating ogre named Alavaka. The Blessed One answered the monster's penetrating questions about life, and it changed its ways and became a follower of the Dharma.

7

Compassion's Ripeness

IN THE TWENTIETH year, when the Buddha was fifty-five years old, he decided henceforth to spend all rainy seasons retreats at Shravasti. Most of those retreats were spent at the Jetavana, donated by Anathapindada, but some of them also at the Purvarama (East Park), which was the gift to the Buddha and Sangha of a woman named Vishakha.

Vishakha was born in the kingdom of Anga. When she was only seven years old the Buddha passed on his wanderings near the village where she was living. At her grandfather's urging, she came forward and presented herself to the Buddha. She approached him, prostrated, and took a seat off to one side. The Blessed One was taken with her refinement and dignified bearing, and in spite of her youth he engaged her in conversation and instructed her in the Dharma. She was such a ready vessel that on that first occasion she attained the first level of realization.

When Vishakha grew to womanhood, she was extraordinarily beautiful. She had iridescent black hair that, when combed out, reached to her calves, and her skin was of an extraordinary radiance and color. Though graceful, she was said to possess the strength of a man.

When she was about seventeen, she was discovered by a group of brahmins charged with finding a suitable wife for their master, a young man named Purnavardhana. Under examination by those brahmins, not only did Vishakha shine in her beauty and poise, but she also replied to a casual remark of theirs with a discourse that stunned them with its wit and penetrating intellect.

Her marriage to Purnavardhana was arranged. There was an elaborate wedding, and then, as was customary, she moved into the house of her father-in-law, Mrigara, in Shravasti. He was an extremely wealthy man who was devoted to the Jain order of naked ascetics, followers of Nirgrantha Jnaniputra. As a result he wanted little to do with the Buddha's bhikshus.

One day the wealthy man was sitting and eating sweet rice porridge from a golden bowl when a begging bhikshu came to the door and stood waiting with his bowl. Vishakha, who was fanning Mrigara, moved out of the way so that he would see the monk. Mrigara saw him but continued eating as though no one were there. After a while, Vishakha told the monk, "Go to the next place, venerable one. My father-in-law is eating stale food."

The assertion that such a grand person as he was eating stale food was taken as a great insult by Mrigara. He flew into a rage and ordered Vishakha expelled from the house. But she had gained the favor of everyone in the household through her generosity and kindness, so no one moved to carry out his order. Then Vishakha remonstrated with Mrigara that it was unconscionable for a woman of good family such as herself to be summarily thrown out in disgrace. She demanded that a neutral group of mediators be called to decide their dispute. As this was customary in such circumstances, Mrigara had little to object to. When the mediators came, Vishakha explained to them that when she saw her father-in-law eating rich food while ignoring the bhikshu, she thought to herself, "Without doing anything of merit in the present life, he sits there consuming the fruits of meritorious deeds of the past." That, she said, was the meaning of her remark about stale food.

The mediators were impressed and found in her favor. They told Mrigara he had no right to expel her. However, Vishakha for her part indicated that now that she had upheld her honor, she no longer wished to remain. And she made ready her departure. This reversal brought Mrigara to a change of heart. He now pleaded with Vishakha to remain and not upset the household. At last she agreed to do so, but on the condition that he would permit her to act as she wished regarding her spiritual convictions. Mrigara agreed to these terms, and Vishakha wasted no time in inviting the Buddha and the Sangha to the wealthy man's house for a meal.

Mrigara was too curious to stay away from the gathering, but to maintain a semblance of loyalty to Nirgrantha's ascetics, he listened to the Buddha's teaching from behind a screen. The screen, however, did nothing to diminish the power of the Blessed One's words. Mrigara was so directly touched by the discourse that he attained the first stage of realization on the spot, and realized that all that is subject to arising is subject to cessation. Afterward his gratitude to Vishakha knew no bounds. And before everyone he proclaimed that because she had shaken him from his ignorance and brought him to the true path, he wished that she should henceforth be regarded as his mother.

Vishakha became a great patron of the Sangha. She donated the great vihara to the Sangha in the vicinity of Shravasti that was called the Purvarama, the Eastern Park. She was also frequently called upon to mediate disputes between bhikshunis. She was often present when the Buddha taught and on other important Sangha occasions. And the Blessed One and the bhikshus and bhikshunis nearly always referred to her as Mrigara's mother.

It was in the twentieth year after his enlightenment that the Tatha-gata decided to appoint Ananda as his permanent personal attendant. He explained that he was getting old and that his constantly changing attendants did not always know their duties well; they sometimes even made matters difficult for him. It would be a help and a relief to him, he said, if Ananda would accept this post. The latter accepted under eight conditions that he felt would make him less of a burden to his master but also ensure that he could be effective in his duties. Thus Ananda was to be in nearly constant attendance on the Tathagata for twenty-five years, until the latter's death, or parinirvana.

IT WAS ALSO in the twentieth year after his enlightenment that the Blessed One converted Angulimala. Angulimala was a murderous bandit who lived in the neighborhood of Shravasti. He murdered people one after the other and strung a finger of each victim on a cord that he wore around his neck. Hence his name, which means "finger necklace."

One day the Buddha took his bowl and outer robe and went into Shravasti for alms. When he had returned and eaten, he put his sleeping place in order and set off toward Angulimala's territory. There was a road running through that territory that was no longer traveled because of people's fear of Angulimala. As the Buddha walked along this road, the few people he encountered warned him not to go any further, because if he did he would certainly fall prey to the fierce bandit. The Buddha did not respond to these people, but merely continued walking. "Bands of up to forty men have gone up that road, and still Angulimala killed them all. Turn back!" people warned. But the Buddha continued on until he was quite alone on the road. Just then Angulimala was surveying the road from a wooded hillside. He saw the Buddha and said to himself, "This is really amazing. Armed men have come along here in large bands, and I've done them all in. Now here comes this monk all by himself. Why shouldn't I kill him too?"

So Angulimala buckled on his weapons, charged down to the road, and started running after the Buddha. But to his astonishment he found that no matter how fast he ran, he could not catch up with the Blessed One, though the latter was walking at a normal pace. Angulimala thought, "This is really amazing. I've outrun galloping horses, running elephants, and even fleet-footed deer. Why can't I catch this monk who is just ambling along!"

In frustration, Angulimala halted and shouted after the Tathagata, "Stop there, monk! Stop!"

"I have stopped," said the Blessed One. "You should stop too!"

"How can you say you've stopped when you're still walking? And how can you tell me to stop when I already have?" shouted the bandit.

"I have stopped forever doing violence to beings," said the Buddha, "whereas you go on doing violence to nearly every creature you meet. Why don't you stop too?"

When Angulimala heard these words and beheld the Tathagata regarding him serenely from just beyond his grasp, the ferocious bandit suddenly saw the situation just as the Buddha saw it. Then and there he vowed in his heart to renounce evil. He tore off his weapons and threw them in a ditch. Then he fell down at the Blessed One's feet and asked him to accept him into homelessness. And then and there the Blessed One said, "Come, bhikshu. The Dharma has been properly proclaimed. Live the holy life for the complete ending of suffering." This made Angulimala a monk.

The Blessed One then set out for Shravasti with Angulimala as his attendant. When he got there, he went to the Jetavana. At that time large numbers of people were gathering daily at King Prasenajit's palace, clamoring for the ferocious bandit Angulimala to be brought to justice. At length, the king gathered five hundred armed men and set out to capture the bandit, but as he had little hope of succeeding, he stopped first at the Jetavana to discuss his problem with the Buddha. When he had finished explaining, the Blessed One asked him, "What would you do if you found out that Angulimala has given up killing and stealing and has devoted himself to the holy life as a bhikshu?"

"Why, I suppose I would pay homage to him and offer him alms," said the king, "but how could that ever happen with a ghastly scoundrel like that?"

The Blessed One stretched out his arm and pointed out Angulimala, who was sitting nearby. "There he is right there," said the Blessed One.

The king started up with fright, but the Buddha told him, "There is nothing to fear." After a short time, the king regained his calm, and he went over to where Angulimala was sitting. The king bowed to him and engaged him in polite conversation. Then finally he requested to be allowed to provide him with food, robes, and medicine, as had then become customary for great patrons. But Angulimala was following a particularly strict rule at that time, which required him to continue begging and to wear a robe pieced together from rags, so he politely declined the king's offer. Then the king returned to the Buddha and, placing his palms together, praised him, using a phrase that was often applied to the Buddha afterward. "You are truly a tamer of untamable beings!" he said.

In the ensuing period, Angulimala remained close to the Buddha and received his instructions. When the time was ripe, he retired into the forest to meditate in earnest. In no long time, the venerable former bandit and murderer became one of the arhats.

SOME MONTHS LATER, when the Blessed One was living near Catuma in the Shakyan country, Shariputra and Maudgalyayana arrived at the place where he was with a party of five hundred bhikshus. Quite a hubbub arose as the newly arrived monks greeted the ones who were already there, unpacked their things, and set up their places. The Buddha called Ananda and asked him what all the noise was. Ananda explained, and the Blessed One told Ananda to request the leaders of the community to come to him. They came and prostrated and sat down at one side. "What was all that noise?" the Buddha asked them. They explained about the arrival of the five hundred bhikshus, and how they had made noise by greeting the bhikshus already there, unpacking, and setting up their places. The Buddha then said, "You are all dismissed. The community is dismissed. You cannot live with me."

So the bhikshus all packed up their things and left the place in a great, slow-moving line. Shakyan householders who were assembled to discuss some civic business saw the crowd of monks moving along and asked them where they were all going. "The Blessed One has dismissed the community. We are leaving," they replied. The Shakyans suggested they sit down and wait for a short time while they went to the Blessed

One and tried to change his mind. So the Shakyans went to the Blessed One and pleaded on behalf of the community. They asked him how it would go with bhikshus who needed guidance if they had no one to guide them. "How can their hearts change if you do not teach them?" they asked.

Moreover, the god Sahampati, who had come to the Buddha after his enlightenment and requested him to turn the wheel of Dharma, now appeared to the Buddha again and pleaded on behalf of the community.

At last the Buddha recalled the community. When they had returned, the Blessed One asked Shariputra what he had thought when the community had been dismissed. He said, "I thought you would dwell by yourself quietly in peace and let the matters of the community drop and we would do the same."

"Not so good," said the Buddha. Then he asked Maudgalyayana what he had thought. He said, "I thought you would dwell quietly in peace and let the matters of the community drop, and Shariputra and I would lead the community."

"Good, good," said the Blessed One. "Either I will lead the Sangha or you and Shariputra will lead it."

At last events did occur in the Sangha that the Buddha deemed suitable occasions for the proclamation of the monastic code of behavior known as the pratimoksha. Sudinna, the son of a wealthy merchant from the vicinity of Vaishali, heard the Buddha teach and asked his parents to permit him to enter homelessness. His parents were hotly opposed to this and reluctantly consented only after Sudinna refused to eat. So Sudinna entered the Sangha, and not long afterward a famine occurred, which made alms food difficult to get. Sudinna hit on the expedient of going to his parents' house for alms. He went once and received alms at the door, and then they invited him the next day for a meal. After the meal, when the time for talking came, Sudinna's mother bewailed the family's plight. If the family remained without an heir, she told her son, on the parents' death, their wealth would revert to the treasury of the Licchavi rulers in Vaishali. She begged Sudinna to meet his former wife in the forest in order to father a child. Sudinna did not see any harm in this, and there was no monastic code to prohibit it, so he went to his wife in the forest three times, and she became pregnant.

Sudinna's wife had a son according to the parents' plan, but their plight was not remedied, for later both wife and son entered homelessness under the Buddha.

Meanwhile, as Sudinna continued with monastic life, his conscience began to trouble him. At last, he went to the Tathagata and recounted the tale of his deeds. The Blessed One called Sudinna "misguided" and upbraided him at length; yet there was no action taken against the young monk, for there was no rule that he had broken.

The Blessed One then convoked an assembly and announced that the time had come for him to lay down a formal code of behavior for the Sangha. This, he said, would restrain the evil-minded, support the virtuous, curb defilements in this life and prevent them in lives to come, and help greatly to establish the Buddha Dharma firmly in the world. The first rule of the code provided that a monk who indulges in sexual intercourse is to be expelled from the community.

After proclaiming the pratimoksha, the Buddha gave further shape to the life of his Sangha by having the code periodically recited rule by rule in a full assembly of bhikshus or bhikshunis. Pauses were made during the recitation to permit public acknowledgment of faults. In this connection, the Blessed One remarked that "rain rots what is kept wrapped up, but not what is uncovered."

THE TATHAGATA HAD long followed a daily routine, which, though not invariable, was fairly constant. The Buddha slept on his right side with his right hand under his head and one foot slightly overlapping the other. This sleeping position of his became known as the lion's posture. It is said that after awakening from sleep before dawn, the Buddha surveyed the panorama of existence with the divine eye and took cognizance of the plight of specific beings. Then he meditated, sitting cross-legged or pacing back and forth in front of his resting place. If he had not been invited for the day's meal by a specific householder, after it was light he would take his bowl and outer robe and walk to the nearest settlement to collect alms. He was usually accompanied by a large following of monks, perhaps several hundred. In collecting alms, he would not go to a specific house where he knew good food might be available, but would start from the end of a given street and proceed house by house. In this way the opportunity for gaining the merit of giving was not reserved for the rich but was spread equally among all. At the door he uttered no request but made his presence known in some inobtrusive way and then stood silently with his bowl in evidence. If alms were given, he accepted in silence anything given in good faith and moved on. If, after a few moments, no alms were given, he passed on in silence. When his bowl was full, he returned to his resting place, washed his feet, and ate his single meal of the day, finishing it before noon.

After finishing the meal, he sat outside near his resting place and gave brief instruction in the Dharma to anyone who was there. When he finished that, he accomplished such work as receiving people into homelessness or granting full ordination. He then retired to an area closed to the public and gave an exposition of the Dharma for the Sangha alone.

If there was an invitation from a householder for the day's meal, there was no alms round. The Buddha and his attendants arrived at the host's house in time to complete the meal before midday. After the meal, the Blessed One gave teaching to the host, his family, and guests. In such cases, he did not teach again in the early part of the day when he returned to the vihara or the monastic camp.

In the heat of the day, he retired to his private place, a simple house if he was in a monastery, and rested. If he wished, he lay down on his right side and slept for a time in a kind of half sleep in which the thread of awareness is not lost. At dusk, large numbers of lay people gathered to hear the Tathagata teach. To them, he delivered a discourse on the Dharma of an hour or more and responded to questions.

After this the Tathagata might bathe and rest for a short time. Then came the conversations with bhikshus or bhikshunis, individually or in groups, that sometimes lasted far into the night.

It is said that the Tathagata slept very little, perhaps only one hour, and then with unbroken mindfulness. In any case, the time between retirement at night and rising at dawn or before was divided between sleeping on his right side, sitting in meditation, and pacing up and down mindfully in front of his sleeping place.

Of course, when the Blessed One was traveling from place to place, after the alms round much of the day was spent walking, except for the rest period in the hot part of the day.

The Sangha followed its master's example, adopting this daily pattern as closely as possible. Those who were not teachers either listened to teaching or meditated at the times of day when the Tathagata taught. Those who were teachers taught the public and their own students at the times of the day when the Tathagata taught the public and his own bhikshus and bhikshunis. Like the Tathagata himself, any member of the Sangha might for a certain time retire to a solitary place to pursue his or her meditation practice intensively.

On one occasion the Blessed One was staying near Shravasti at the Purvarama vihara donated by Mrigara's mother. It was a posadha day, reserved for the recitation of the pratimoksha and the confessions of the Sangha. The Buddha sat in the great hall of the vihara amid a full convocation of the community. The assembly was waiting for the Tathagata to recite the pratimoksha, and the first watch of the night (which runs until two hours before midnight) had already come to an end. Still the Tathagata sat on in silence. Ananda got to his feet and turned to face him, placing his palms together in the gesture of supplication. "Lord," he said, "it is getting quite late, and the assembly of the Sangha has been sitting for a long time. Please let the Blessed One recite the pratimoksha." Ananda then took his seat.

The Tathagata remained silent.

Much later, at the end of the second watch (which runs until two hours after midnight), Ananda rose to his feet once more. "Lord," he said, "it is getting quite late, and the assembly of the Sangha has been sitting for a long time. Please let the Blessed One recite the pratimoksha."

Once more the Buddha remained silent.

When the third watch was over and dawn was beginning to break, Ananda rose a third time from his seat. "Lord," he said, "it is well on into the night, and the red dawn is just now beginning to bring joy to the face of the darkness. The assembly has been sitting long. Please let the Blessed One recite the pratimoksha."

"The assembly is not pure," said the Blessed One.

Maudgalyayana read the minds of the entire assembly. At length, he found a person who was merely behaving outwardly as a bhikshu but whose mind was full of corrupt and lascivious thoughts, to which he gave free rein. Maudgalyayana went to him and said, "Get up, friend. The Tathagata has seen you. You cannot live in communion with the Sangha." The pretending monk did not respond. Maudgalyayana repeated himself a second and a third time. The offender still neither moved nor spoke. Finally, Maudgalyayana took the man by the arm, forcibly led him to the door, and put him out. Then he approached the Blessed One and said, "Lord, I have removed that person. Please be so kind as to recite the pratimoksha."

"It is truly amazing," said the Blessed One, "how that man waited until he was taken by the arm and removed. I must tell you that I will no longer take part in the posadha. I will no longer recite the pratimoksha. You will have to do this by yourselves. It is impossible for a Tathagata to recite the pratimoksha in an impure assembly."

Then the Blessed One gave a splendid and inspiring discourse on the greatness of the Dharma and the code of monastic discipline.

ONCE WHEN THE Blessed One was on the way from Rajagriha to Vaishali, he observed a great number of bhikshus traveling on the roads laden down with bundles of clothing. He thought, "These bhikshus are so easily drawn into luxury and excess. It seems I must limit the number of robes each bhikshu may possess." When the Blessed One arrived at Vaishali, he sat up through the night outdoors during the eight coldest nights of the year. At first he wore only one robe and did not feel cold. Then he got cold and put on a second robe. As the night wore on, he felt no cold. Then he did feel cold and put on a third robe. He felt no cold for a long time. Then, as dawn showed its first rays, he felt cold again and had to put on a fourth robe. Then he was not cold anymore.

From this the Blessed One concluded that even bhikshus sensitive to cold could survive with the customary triple robe. So he made a rule saying that only the triple robe was permissible: an outer robe of double thickness pieced together from patches, one inner robe, and one cloth to wrap around the lower body.

ONCE WHEN THE Blessed One was staying at the Vulture Peak mountain near Rajagriha, King Bimbisara was calling representatives from all the little districts throughout Magadha to come to the capital. The leading family of one district had a son named Shrona whom they had so successfully sheltered from any crude effort that hair had grown on the soles of his feet. This renowned evidence of their son's delicacy became known to the king, and he asked that Shrona be brought to the convocation of representatives at the palace so he could see the phenomenon for himself. Shrona was brought on a litter to the palace and sat cross-legged at the front of the assembly so that the king could see the fine hair growing on the soles of his feet.

Then the king gave a talk to the assembled district representatives, instructing them on the aims and proper conduct of life. Then he told them, "I have given you instruction on the matters of this mundane life. Now go, all of you, and pay homage to the Blessed One at Vulture Peak Mountain, and perhaps he will instruct you in the matters transcending life and death."

So it happened that Shrona was among those who went to hear the

Tathagata teach at Vulture Peak Mountain that day. The Buddha instructed the assembled representatives and then gave them all the triple refuge. Shrona was so inspired that at the first opportunity, he made his way to the Buddha and requested to be received into homelessness. The Buddha received him, and Shrona became a bhikshu.

He was a very eager student and soon retired into the forest to practice meditation intensively. He strived so mightily to attain realization that the pacing-back-and-forth area in front of his meditation seat was soaked in blood from the ruins of his delicate feet. He was beginning to get discouraged. Knowing how it was with him, the Buddha paid Shrona a visit. When Shrona saw him coming, he quickly prepared a seat for him and then sat down off to one side.

The Buddha asked him, "Weren't you just thinking to yourself that even though you are pursuing the goal very diligently, at least as energetically as any of my disciples, still realization eludes you, so perhaps there is no hope for you in this endeavor?"

"Yes, lord, I was thinking that."

"Were you thinking that since your family has tremendous wealth, perhaps you could do more good by returning to the householder's life and employing that wealth meritoriously?"

"Yes, lord, I was thinking that."

"Weren't you an excellent vina player when you were still in the householder's life?"

"Yes, lord."

"When the strings of your vina were tuned too tight, did they sound good?"

"No, lord. They were squeaky and harsh and hard to work with the fingers."

"When they were too loose, how did they sound then?"

"Not good then either, lord. Slack and dull."

"Was it when the strings were neither too tight nor too loose that they responded well to your fingers and made beautiful music? Is that right, Shrona?"

"Yes, lord, that is just the case."

"It is the same in meditation, Shrona. Do you understand?"

"I understand, lord. Not too loose and not too tight."

"Don't try too hard, Shrona, and don't give up either."

"Yes, lord."

ONCE THE BLESSED One was inspecting all the living spaces at a particular vihara with Ananda alongside him. They came to one dwelling where there was a monk lying covered in his own urine and feces. When the Buddha saw that, he talked with the man and found out that he had dysentery and that no one was taking care of him, because the other bhikshus had simply given him up for dead. Then the Blessed One told Ananda to fetch water, and together they washed the man. Then the Buddha took him at the head and Ananda at the feet, and they lifted him onto a bed and made him as comfortable as they could.

Then the Blessed One called the bhikshus of that place together and asked them if they knew there was a man lying sick there with dysentery. "We know there is, lord," they said.

"And why is no one taking care of him?" he asked.

"He is no longer any use to the community," they responded.

"In the Sangha," the Blessed One told them, "we have no mother or father or relatives to look after us. If we do not look after one another, who will look after us?" Then he made it a rule that if someone is sick, his instructor or his teacher should look after him, or someone who has the same teacher or instructor, until he either recovers or dies. He made it a serious offense to overlook this rule.

YEAR AFTER YEAR the Buddha spent the rainy season at Shravasti and then wandered the central Gangetic plain, for the most part teaching daily, converting lay followers and giving them the triple refuge, and receiving others into the monastic Sangha. Year by year he refined the formulation of various aspects of his doctrine. Case by case, only when occasioned by specific occurrences, he added rules to the pratimoksha until there were two hundred and twenty-seven rules for bhikshus and three hundred and thirty-eight for bhikshunis. The Sangha benefited from the favor of great kings such as King Bimbisara of Magadha and King Prasenajit and countless wealthy householders, so that gradually it came to possess well-appointed viharas throughout the land, and especially many in the neighborhood of Vaishali, Shravasti, and Rajagriha, cities which the Blessed One particularly frequented.

8

Devadatta

IN THE THIRTY-SEVENTH YEAR after the Buddha's enlightenment, when the great sage of the Shakyas was seventy-two years old, there arose a serious menace to his life and the unity of the Sangha. There was a bhikshu named Devadatta, the son of Suprabuddha, the Shakyan noble who had been swallowed by the earth in Kapilavistu. Devadatta's mother was an aunt of the Buddha's. He was thus both the Blessed One's cousin and his brother-in-law. It will be recalled that he entered homelessness along with the Shakyan princes who came to the Buddha with their barber, Upali. Unlike the others, he had never attained any of the stages of realization. Nevertheless, he was genial and charming and an exemplary bhikshu, a well-liked person with an extensive following within the Sangha. Moreover, though unable to attain a clear vision of dependent arising and the Four Noble Truths, he had become proficient in the exercise of supernormal powers.

Once, when he was meditating alone in retreat, with no apparent antecedent the idea arose in him of gaining fame and power. Instead of letting the idea pass by, Devadatta nurtured it and began to scheme how he might achieve this goal. He hit upon the idea of winning the devotion of Prince Ajatashatru, King Bimbisara's son and heir. So he took the form of a naked child garlanded about with coiling snakes and appeared in Prince Ajatashatru's lap. The prince was struck with mortal terror, but Devadatta spoke to him soothingly. "Calm yourself, my prince," he said. "Do you know who I am? I am Devadatta." Then he showed himself in his own form, wearing his robes and carrying his begging bowl.

The astonished prince conceived a kind of worship for Devadatta. He attended daily upon the ambitious monk and had him lavishly supplied with the finest food, which was carried to him by trains of richly liveried servants. With the prince making this great show of discipleship, Devadatta quickly grew in fame and prestige among the people of Rajagriha. He gloried in this new power, and even greater ambitions came to possess his mind. He thought now of displacing the Buddha and taking over for himself the leadership of the Sangha.

But as these thoughts took shape in Devadatta's mind and firmed into an intention, his supernormal powers vanished as though they had never been.

At this time, pursuing the normal course of his wanderings, the Tathagata arrived in Rajagriha. Monks told him of Devadatta's rise to power, how Ajatashatru had elevated him to almost divine status, and how Devadatta had failed to set these honors aside. The Blessed One responded that the monks should not begrudge Devadatta his worldly renown, but allowed that the situation was not good for Devadatta personally. The longer it lasted, he said, the more likely it was to lead to the errant monk's destruction.

One day the Buddha was teaching the Dharma to a great gathering of people near the city. Many Rajagrihan notables, including the king, were present, and this was the moment Devadatta chose to approach the Buddha, prostrate himself to him, and in a voice all could hear, address him as follows: "The Blessed One is now old, aged, advanced in years, in the last stage of life, nearing the end. The Blessed One should rest now. The Blessed One should have respite from his work and spend his days in blissful contemplation of the Dharma. For that reason, let the Blessed One hand over leadership of the Sangha to me. I will lead the Sangha well."

"Abandon this idea, Devadatta," said the Buddha. "Do not aspire to lead the Sangha."

Devadatta ignored the Buddha's answer and loudly repeated his own words. The Buddha met them with the same response. Yet a third time Devadatta uttered his brazen formula. A third time the Buddha replied, "I would not give over the leadership of the Sangha even to the great bhikshus Shariputra and Maudgalyayana. Why then would I give it over to you, who are like something bad-tasting in the mouth that needs to be spit out?"

This was a bitter humiliation for Devadatta. The Buddha had praised Shariputra and Maudgalyayana and degraded him in the same breath. Yet he preserved the appearance of respect for the Tathagata by bowing to him with palms together and turning his right side in departing.

Following this incident, the Blessed One announced in a gathering of the Sangha that a public denunciation of Devadatta was needed. It was to be proclaimed in Rajagriha that Devadatta, though formerly an estimable bhikshu, had now changed and was no longer representative of the Sangha. Thus the Sangha henceforth dissociated itself from any responsibility for Devadatta's acts. Then the Blessed One turned to Shariputra and told him he must be the one to proclaim this in Rajagriha.

"But, Blessed One, until now I have praised Devadatta to the people, telling them how good and powerful he was. How can I go now and denounce him?"

"Did you formerly speak the truth in praising Devadatta?"

"Yes, lord, I did."

"Would you also be speaking the truth now in denouncing him?"

"I would, lord. That is so, lord."

So Shariputra went into Rajagriha with a company of monks and publicly denounced Devadatta. Different reactions among the people were quick to emerge. Some said that the public denunciation was motivated by jealousy of Devadatta on the part of the Buddha's followers. Others said, "If the Blessed One is having Devadatta denounced, there must be something terribly wrong with Devadatta."

Devadatta's response was to go to Prince Ajatashatru and say, "The two of us together can hold total power. Why wait for the old ones to die? If you wait, you may die before you become king. Therefore, kill Bimbisara and take the crown. Then I will kill the Blessed One and become the Buddha!"

Ajatashatru thought, "Devadatta has so much power, he must know what is right." So he took a knife and hid it under his clothing and tried to sneak into Bimbisara's apartments. But the king's guards caught the prince and questioned him. Ajatashatru admitted that he had meant to kill his father and admitted as well that Devadatta had put him up to the deed. The king had his son brought before him and asked him, "Why do you want to kill me, son?"

"Because I want the kingdom, my lord."

"In that case, you shall have it," said Bimbisara. Shortly thereafter he abdicated in favor of Ajatashatru, keeping only a small share of the royal wealth. Later, grown still more greedy for power, Ajatashatru came to begrudge his father even the crumb of wealth and power he kept for himself. He had Bimbisara thrown into a dungeon, where the former king was allowed to starve to death.

As soon as Ajatashatru was king, Devadatta went to him and asked him to command some of his soldiers to kill the Buddha. Ajatashatru called for some soldiers and placed them under Devadatta's orders. Devadatta devised a complex plan. He told one man where "the monk Gautama" was living and ordered the man to go there and kill him and return by a certain path. He posted two men on that path and told them to kill the returning murderer. Having done so, these two men were to return by a certain path, where he posted four men who were ordered to kill the two. Then, in the same way, eight men were ordered to kill the four, and sixteen the eight.

The man who was to kill the Buddha armed himself with sword and bow and went to carry out his task. But as he neared where the Buddha was, he began to feel intimidation. When he got closer, intimidation turned to fear. At last, when he was quite close, he froze with terror and could go no further. The Blessed One saw him and said, "Come near, friend, do not be afraid." The man cast off his weapons and threw himself at the Blessed One's feet. He confessed what he had meant to do and begged the Buddha's forgiveness.

The Buddha told him he had indeed done wrong, but since he had seen his fault and acknowledged it, it could be forgiven. "That is how one may grow in the Dharma," he explained, "by seeing one's confusion and acknowledging it as such." Then he gave him progressive instruction until the man had a clear vision of the Dharma and realized that everything subject to arising is subject to cessation. The Buddha went on instructing the man, and he attained the level of independent knowledge that no longer needs confirmation from others. He begged the Blessed One to receive him as his follower.

Then the Tathagata told him, "Friend, don't go back by that path, go back by this other one."

The two men who were to kill the first one eventually got tired of waiting and went to see what had happened to him. They followed the path until they came to where the Buddha was sitting under a tree. They prostrated to him and sat down off to one side. The Buddha then instructed them, and they too asked to become his followers. Then he pointed out to them a harmless path to return by. Matters went similarly with the groups of four, eight, and sixteen men, who all encountered the Buddha in succession.

When Devadatta learned how his plan had gone, he decided to kill the Buddha himself. The vengeance-bent bhikshu went in search of the Tathagata and at last spied him in the distance, pacing back and forth in the shade of the great rock at the top of Vulture Peak Mountain. Devadatta climbed the rock from behind and dislodged a great boulder and sent it tumbling down on the Blessed One. But the boulder caught fast between two rocks just above where the Blessed One was pacing, and the only harm he suffered was from a splinter of the great boulder that deeply penetrated his foot.

This wound caused the Tathagata a great deal of pain, not only in the foot but through his whole body. He bore the pain mindfully and without complaint but had to retire to his house and rest for a few days. This he did lying with unbroken awareness on his right side. As he lay there, Mara came to him and chided him for his indulgence. The Blessed One, however, immediately saw who it was, and as soon as Mara knew he had been caught, he disappeared.

After two days the Buddha was disturbed by a cacophony of jumbled voices coming from outside his house. He called Ananda for an explanation. The latter informed him that the Sangha had learned that attempts were being made on the Blessed One's life, instigated by Devadatta. Now more and more bhikshus and bhikshunis were arriving to circle his house, chanting protective incantations. The Blessed One requested Ananda to call them all together. Then he said to them, "Bhikshus, no tathagata can be killed by another's violence. When a tathagata dies, another's violence is not the cause. All of you may return to your places. A tathagata requires no protection."

Meanwhile Devadatta had conceived another scheme for killing the Buddha. In Rajagriha there was a crazed, man-killing elephant named Nalagiri that was kept by the king for purposes of war. To maintain his evil temper, the elephant's daily water supply was laced with large quantities of liquor. On a day, when Devadatta knew that the Buddha would be coming along a certain street for alms, he bribed the great bull elephant's keepers to double its ration of liquor and let it out into the street at the right moment. Nalagiri was released and saw the Blessed One beginning his alms round at the far end of the street. He raised his trunk and trumpeted, then charged, berserk, down the street, bent on the destruction of that tiny robed figure.

The monks with the Tathagata saw the elephant in the distance and exhorted him to get out of the street. "It is the mad man-killing elephant Nalagiri!" they cried.

"I told you just the other day," said the Buddha matter-of-factly, "that it is impossible to kill a tathagata by violence. There is nothing to fear."

Urgently the monks pleaded with the Buddha to get out of the street. He paid them no heed and calmly continued walking. People gathered at the windows of the great houses of the wealthy and the small houses of the poor to watch the impending crisis. Some said, "Oh, dear, the great monk who is so beautiful to look at will be mashed and mutilated by that crazy Nalagiri!" Others said, "Soon one great tusker will be clashing with another."

Some of the monks with the Buddha fell back. Ananda tried to get in front of the Blessed One so as to take the brunt of the charge. The Buddha took Ananda by the arm and drew him firmly out of the way. Then the Blessed One embraced the charging beast in a great field of lovingkindness. The crazed elephant lowered its trunk and slowed its charge. It came to a confused halt and tossed its huge head from side to side. Then it came on at a slow trot and halted before the Tathagata. The Buddha reached up with his right hand and stroked Nalagiri between the eyes. Then he spoke to him softly in a kind of croon: "O great tusker, do not kill another tusker, a bull elephant, a tathagata. Such an act would bring you an endless destiny of unhappiness. Give up your conceit and madness, great elephant. Tread the path that will bring you future happiness." After the Buddha had spoken to him for a few moments in this way, Nalagiri gathered up dust from about the Tathagata's feet with his trunk and placed it on top of his own head. Then he withdrew, walking backward. Only far down the street did he turn and trot back to the stable. There he stood peacefully in his stall.

Soon a jingle was making the rounds of the streets:

> *Some tamers tame with whips,*
> *With sticks and goads others go,*
> *But the Buddha has a tusker tamed*
> *And never struck a blow.*

After this incident there was general condemnation of Devadatta's base attacks on the great monk whose might and wisdom were so clear to see. Most of the discredited schemer's followers in the city fell away. Ajatashatru, too, no longer found it seemly to support him. But still Devadatta kept a fair number of adherents within the Sangha itself.

With his lavish food supply in the city cut off, Devadatta and his followers now thrust themselves upon ordinary householders, coming in large numbers to a single house for their daily meal. As this caused hardship and stirred up resentment among the people, some bhikshus reported the matter to the Buddha. The Blessed One was obliged to make a new ruling limiting the number of monks who could accept an invitation at one house to three.

This ruling by the Buddha led Devadatta to his next plan. Judging that further physical attack on the Buddha was futile, he now conspired with his followers to cause a schism in the Sangha. His supporters were skeptical at first of being able to overcome the Blessed One, but Devadatta devised a new plan that succeeded in drawing them in.

Knowing that the people idealized self-denial as a high spiritual goal, he went to the Buddha and proposed five points of strict behavior for Sangha members: they must keep to the forests and never live in a settled place; eat only begged alms food and never accept meal invitations; wear only robes pieced together from refuse rags and never accept a gift of cloth; dwell only outdoors and never in shelters; and never eat fish or meat. He proposed that violation of any of these rules be met with expulsion from the Sangha.

The Buddha rejected these rules as too extreme. He ruled that Sangha members were free to dwell in forests or villages, eat alms food or accept invitations, wear refuse-rag robes or accept cloth as they chose. They could dwell either outdoors or in shelters for eight months of the year, but must take shelter during the rainy season. Meat and fish could be eaten if it was not seen, heard, or suspected to have been killed expressly for the eater.

This was the kind of ruling Devadatta had been waiting for. He and his followers at once set talk going in the Sangha that set one faction against another. They depicted their own party under Devadatta's leadership as that of the upholders of the strict and pure Dharma, and implied that those who followed the Buddha were slack, lovers of luxury. "Come to us," they said. "We will follow Devadatta and uphold the five righteous rules." Many followed Devadatta, because they thought greater self-denial was the higher and more noble course.

When the Blessed One heard about this, he spoke with Devadatta personally and asked him if he was really, as it seemed, intentionally trying to destroy the unity of the Sangha. Devadatta acknowledged that he was. The Buddha tried to bring him to reason. He told Devadatta that he had already laid up horrendous karmic results for himself by shedding the blood of a tathagata when the rock splinter pierced his foot. "Creating a schism in the Sangha is a very grave thing," he told him, "but reuniting it brings much merit."

This kind of talk had no effect on Devadatta. Shortly after this meeting he let it be known that on the next scheduled posadha day, he would hold the ceremony separately, with his own sangha, and recite his own version of the pratimoksha. "I will lead the community," he said, "and make the judgments on infractions of the code." Then he and his men went among the Sangha members and tried to persuade as many of them as possible to come and follow Devadatta. "All those in favor of the righteous five points should join us," they said.

At that time there were five hundred bhikshus from the region of Vaishali who were new entrants into the Sangha. Those five hundred were impressed by the stricter code, and thinking, "This is the true teaching," they decided to follow Devadatta. Thus he succeeded in creating a schism in the Sangha.

The next day Devadatta and his accomplices set out for Gaya-shirsha with their following of five hundred new bhikshus. Shariputra and Maudgalyayana brought word of this to the Buddha. The Buddha asked his two leading disciples if they did not feel compassion for the five hundred bhikshus who had fallen under Devadatta's sway.

"We do, lord," they replied.

"Then go and save them before it's too late," he said. The two immediately left for Gayashirsha. After they had gone, a monk standing near the Buddha broke into tears. The Buddha asked him, "Why are you crying, monk?"

"Once Shariputra and Maudgalyayana get to Gayashirsha, they will be won over by Devadatta, and they too will stand against the Blessed One," he said amid his sobs.

"Peace, bhikshu. Do not imagine that that is a possibility. What will happen will be quite different from that."

When the two great disciples of the Buddha arrived in Gayashirsha, Devadatta was sitting teaching the doctrine to the full assembly of his followers. He saw the two foremost disciples of the Buddha coming and said to those around him, "See there. I have proclaimed the Dharma well. Even Shariputra and Maudgalyayana have come to join us."

Devadatta's chief advisor bent over to whisper in his ear. "Send them away, lord. Their intentions toward us are evil."

"Abandon such cowardly thoughts, my friend," Devadatta replied. "Welcome them, for they have come to support my doctrine and leadership."

When the two disciples were in speaking range, Devadatta called out to Shariputra and invited him to come forward and share his seat. Shariputra politely declined. The two disciples sat down off to one side. Then Devadatta resumed his teaching. He talked long into the night, occasionally making use of one or another of the Buddha's characteristic gestures, and he waxed eloquent on various details of the doctrine. Sometime after the beginning of the second watch, he paused in his teaching and spoke to the Buddha's disciple. "Shariputra," he said, "the

Sangha is still free from fatigue and drowsiness. Perhaps some words of Dharma might come to your mind. I have some pain in my back, so I will rest awhile."

"As you say, friend," said Shariputra.

Then Devadatta folded his outer robe in four and lay down on his right side in the lion's pose, with one hand under his head and one foot slightly overlapping the other. But Devadatta was tired. His attention lapsed, and he fell fast asleep.

Shariputra began teaching the assembly, giving progressive instruction. With his subtle perception of the real meaning behind the words of teaching, he was able to speak a direct message that removed the veils from the understanding of the new bhikshus. After he had taught them for a time, Maudgalyayana took the teacher's seat and taught them in his turn. Easily reading the minds of the assembled, he attuned his message to what they were thinking. Before the end of the second watch, between the two of them, the two great disciples were able to bring most of those five hundred new bhikshus to a pure vision of the Dharma in which they saw that whatever is subject to arising is subject to cessation. Then the two disciples of the Buddha stood up, and Shariputra said, "We are returning now to the Blessed One. Let all those who are follower's of the Buddha's Dharma come with us."

Then the whole assembly joined Shariputra and Maudgalyayana without hesitation, and they followed them to the Venuvana where the Buddha was staying.

Meanwhile, Devadatta's chief advisor woke the slumbering usurper and said, "I told you didn't I!? Shariputra and Maudgalyayana have taken the five hundred bhikshus with them, and they have all gone back to the Buddha!" When Devadatta heard this, he was so stricken and mortified that hot blood gushed from his mouth. This was a blow from which Devadatta never recovered. Not long after, mortally ill, he tried to go to the Buddha to beg his forgiveness, but before he could reach him, he died.

When Shariputra and Maudgalyayana rejoined the Buddha at the Venuvana, he asked them how they had managed to bring back the errant bhikshus. "My lord," replied Shariputra, "Devadatta did just exactly as the Blessed One sometimes does. After having taught the assembly long into the night, he turned to me and, using your very words, said, 'Shariputra, the Sangha is still free from fatigue and drowsiness. Perhaps some words of Dharma might come to your mind. I have some pain in my back, so I will rest awhile.' Then he folded his outer robe in four and lay down on his right side just as the Blessed One does. But rather than remaining mindful, he simply fell asleep. So Maudgalyayana and I were able to speak to those misguided bhikshus and bring them to their senses."

After that the Blessed One addressed the assembled Sangha: "Once, bhikshus, there were some elephants living near a big pond in a forest. They would go into the pond and pull up lotus stalks with their trunks; and when they had washed them quite clean, they would chew them up and swallow them free from mud. That was good for both their looks and their health, and they incurred no death or deadly suffering because of that. Then some young calves, uninstructed by those elephants, went into the pond and pulled up lotus stalks with their trunks; but instead of washing them quite clean, they chewed them up and swallowed them along with the mud. That was not good for either their looks or their health, and they incurred death and deadly suffering because of that. So too, bhikshus, Devadatta will die miserably through imitating me.

> "Aping me wretchedly he dies
> Like the calf that also eats the mud
> Trying to copy the Tusker eating lotus
> Watchful in the river
> Shaking off soil."[18]

In the time following the demise of Devadatta, Ajatashatru was induced by one of his followers to hear the Buddha teach. Tormented by pangs of conscience and deeply moved by the Blessed One's teaching, the patricide prostrated to the Blessed One, acknowledged his faults, and swore to better himself in the future. Then he asked to be accepted as the Buddha's follower, and the Blessed One gave him the triple refuge.

9

Last Years

As the Buddha grew older, there was little to differentiate his activities from those of his younger days. Except for the rainy season, he continued to walk the dusty Indian roads, traveling the country watered by the Ganges and its tributaries. He continued to go into the towns and villages himself to gather alms, and teaching continued unabated. Yet in his late seventies, his health began to deteriorate. His back grew bent, his skin grew wrinkled and lost some of its fine radiance, and his senses lost some of their sharpness. He would sit in the late afternoon after rising from the midday retreat, warming his back in the setting sun. Ananda would often massage his limbs to ease the muscles.

At that time, Nirgrantha Jnaniputra — the leader of the naked ascetics, the Jains — died. A great schism split his followers in two factions, and even the lay followers were caught up in the bitter struggle between them. This situation caused monks to ask the Buddha how dissension between factions could be avoided at the time of his own death. The question was purveyed by Ananda. The Buddha reeled off a long list of teachings he had given. Then he said, "Ananda, of all these teachings that I have directly known and taught, can you find two monks anywhere in the Sangha who would be in disagreement on how to describe any one of them?"

"No, lord," replied Ananda. "But when you are gone, there might be many disagreements among those who now meekly follow about the pratimoksha or the proper mode of livelihood for monks."

"Disagreement on those matters are insignificant, Ananda," said the Buddha. "But should there be disagreements on matters of doctrine or practice, that would indeed be a misfortune."

ONE OF THE Buddha's great royal patrons, King Bimbisara, was now gone. His successor, Ajatashatru, was greedy for territory and continually warring with great Koshala or the smaller republics. But King Prasenajit of Koshala, who was the same age as the Buddha, became more and more devoted to the Tathagata as time went on. Since the Blessed One spent a large part of every year in Shravasti, King Prasenajit would come to see him often. On one of his visits, he complained to the Blessed One that he was growing ever so weary of the affairs of state. Then the Blessed One asked him, "What if, great king, one of your trusted men came to you and told you a huge mountain of earth, immense and unstoppable, was advancing toward you rapidly from the east, crushing everything in its path? Then suppose that other trusted men came from each of the other three directions and reported to you that there was such a huge mountain of earth coming from each of those other directions too, crushing everything before it. What would you do?"

"What else would there be to do at such a moment but follow the Dharma, cultivate what is wholesome, and accumulate merit?" replied the old king.

"In just the same way as those mountains of earth, old age and death are closing in on us right now," the Buddha continued, "so what else can we do but follow the Dharma, cultivate what is wholesome, and accumulate merit?"

In addition to his troublesome wars with his nephew Ajatashatru, King Prasenajit had to come to grips with increasing challenges within his own kingdom, some of them stemming from his son Virudhaka, who was eyeing the throne with impatience. In the wake of an attempted palace coup, Prasenajit mistakenly had one of his generals, who he believed had plotted against him, assassinated. When he later learned that the general had been loyal, it was a hard blow to the old man. Then Queen Mallika died, the brilliant woman who had been his consort, loyal companion, and counselor. This finally broke the old man's will to govern. Having no more taste for the capital, he took to wandering about the country more or less aimlessly with a large retinue of state. Often, when he happened to be somewhere near the Blessed One, he would go to see him.

One day, when Prasenajit and the Blessed One had both reached eighty years of age, the king was out viewing a pleasure park in the countryside, accompanied by his chief minister, Dirghacharayana, a nephew of the general whom he had erroneously had killed. The king had dismounted from his carriage and was taking a walk when he saw a beautiful and quiet grove that reminded him strongly of the places the Buddha and his monks would choose for their meditation retreats. So strongly was he reminded of the Buddha that he at once asked Dirghacharayana if he knew where the Blessed One might be just then. The chief minister informed him that the Blessed One was staying near a village not far away, "close enough to reach before dusk, your majesty."

"Let us go at once," said the king. "How wonderful it would be to see the Blessed One again!"

The royal party indeed reached the village while there was still daylight and drove on toward the park where the Blessed One was staying. When the carriage could go no further, the king and his minister dismounted and continued on foot until they came to an area where they found monks walking around. The king asked one of the monks where the Buddha could be found. The monk pointed out a house that was quite near. "Go up on the veranda very quietly," he said. "Then cough and tap lightly on the door. The Blessed One will let you in."

Then the king took off his crown and sword and all his other emblems of royalty, gave them to Dirghacharayana to hold, and approached the Buddha's house. Dirghacharayana thought to himself, "So I must wait here while the king has a private conference with the Blessed One. Could it have been after a little session like this that the king had my uncle killed? Am I next?"

The king followed the monk's instructions. He coughed and tapped softly on the door. Indeed the Buddha came to the door and admitted him. The king prostrated to the Blessed One. Then lovingly he took the Buddha's feet between his hands and covered them with kisses. As he kissed his feet he repeated several times, "I am Prasenajit, king of Koshala, I am Prasenajit, king of Koshala."

One might have thought the old man witless, but what followed showed otherwise. The Buddha asked him to what he owed the extreme honor he was being shown by the great king. Prasenajit then took a seat and, in answer, delivered himself of an extraordinary and lengthy discourse, full of wisdom, eloquence, and affection, praising the Buddha, the Dharma, and the Sangha. "And as though that were not enough," he concluded, "you are a warrior noble and I am a warrior noble, and you are eighty and I am eighty. And that is why I do extreme honor to the Buddha and am so full of friendliness." Then King Prasenajit took his leave, saying that he had much to do.

After he had gone, the Buddha spoke to the bhikshus who were in attendance: "Bhikshus, King Prasenajit has just raised great monuments to the Dharma. Note his words and remember them, for they are wholesome words."

King Prasenajit went to rejoin Dirghacharayana, but the latter was nowhere to be seen. When the king had gone inside, the chief minister had departed with the crown and other royal insignia. He rode away with these and all the royal retinue and went straight to the king's heir, Virudhaka. He urged the latter in forcible terms to ascend the throne at once. To Prasenajit, he sent only a woman of the palace with a horse and sword and the message that if the king valued his life, he would not return to Shravasti.

Prasenajit decided to take refuge in Rajagriha. In the last war between the Koshalans and Magadhans, Prasenajit had gained the victory and captured Ajatashatru. Rather than having him executed as expected, since Ajatashatru was his nephew he had spared his life and allowed him to remain on the Magadhan throne. Now, he thought, Ajatashatru would show him favor. He rode to Rajagriha and took lodging at an inn outside the city walls. He sent his traveling companion to bring word of his presence to the Magadhan king. But while waiting at the inn, he ate some unaccustomedly coarse food, was taken ill, and died before Ajatashatru could come to his aid.

IN HIS LAST YEAR, though flagging physically, the Buddha continued to wander and teach. His teachings, however, now took on a synoptic quality that seemed designed to fix the doctrine clearly for the future. Concentrated talks with repeated enumerations of basic doctrinal points were the order of the day. Again and again now, he returned in his talks to the relationship of discipline (shila), meditation (samadhi), and knowledge that sees things as they really are (prajna). Meditation, he taught, must be supported by discipline, and knowledge must be supported by meditation. The mind illuminated by knowledge that is soaked in discipline and meditation will become liberated from the defilements and obscurations of desire, conceptual views, and ignorance of its own nature. This is what the Buddha told the assembled bhikshus and bhikshunis with tireless frequency in his final months.

During this period the Blessed One stayed for a time near a village called Pataligrama on the southern bank of the Ganges, south of Vaishali. There he taught the Sangha again about discipline, meditation, and knowledge, but focused particularly on the dangers of not having discipline and the benefits of having it. At this time two ministers of Ajatashatru were living at a nearby site where they were supervising the construction of a fortified city to serve in Ajatashatru's wars against the Vrijians. One evening the Buddha gazed out over the fields where they were constructing their city and saw that it was thronged with deities. He told the bhikshus accompanying him that powerful deities influence powerful kings and ministers to build mighty cities in the places where they reside. Then he prophesied an illustrious future for the city being built by Ajatashatru's ministers, which later was called Pataliputra and became the majestic capital of the Magadhan and the Mauryan empires. (It is now the city of Patna, the capital of Bihar, which covers much of the area where the Buddha lived and taught.)

The two ministers invited the Blessed One to a meal, and when it was over he taught them in beautiful language, exhorting them always to provide food for the virtuous Sangha and always to make offerings to the local deities. To the man who makes offerings to the local deities comes good fortune, he said,

> Because their love for him is like
> A mother's love for her own child;
> And when a man is loved by the gods,
> He always sees auspicious things.[19]

The ministers were deeply touched by this encounter, and they decided to mark the place by which the Blessed One left the site of the future city and build a gate there, to be called the Gautama Gate. They also intended to mark the spot where he forded the Ganges on his way north and call it the Gautama Ford. The place where the Buddha left the site indeed came to be called the Gautama Gate. But when he came to the Ganges, the water was too high for fording. People who wanted to cross were busy on the banks looking for anything that might serve as a boat or lashing together odd bits of wood for rafts. The Buddha and the large company of monks accompanying him were standing on the riverbank observing this scene. Then suddenly they vanished and instantly reappeared on the far shore. Looking back at the river, the Buddha remarked that while ordinary people who want to cross the waters are struggling with boats or rafts or building bridges in deep water, the wise have already crossed.

ONE OF THE LAST TIMES the Blessed One visited Vaishali he stayed in the mango-grove park of the renowned state courtesan Amrapali (Keeper of Mangoes). There he taught on the four foundations of mindfulness. Now, Amrapali was a very beautiful, a very intelligent, and a highly cultured woman, so much so that she was regarded by the Vrijians as one of the chief treasures of their realm. When she heard that the Blessed One was staying in her mango grove, she set off at once to see him at the head of a long procession of magnificent state carriages. After prostrating to the Buddha and receiving teaching from him, she invited him and the Sangha to accept the following day's meal from her.

The noble Licchavis, the ruling clan of the Vrijian confederacy, whose city Vaishali was, also heard of the Buddha's arrival. They too drove out to see him in a gorgeous procession of state carriages. They were clothed in their finery, some in blue, with blue makeup and blue jewelry; others in yellow, with yellow makeup and yellow jewelry, and so with the rest in a festival of colors. And each rode in an ornate carriage of matching color. On the way, they met Amrapali, who told them she had invited the Buddha for the following day. When they heard that, they felt they had been beaten to the prize and offered her a hundred thousand pieces of gold to assign the invitation to them. "Not for the whole city!" she replied. Knowing there was no point in bargaining with this powerful woman, they continued on their way. The Buddha saw them coming and said to the bhikshus who were with him, "Those of you who have never yet visited the Heaven of the Thirty-three, look well at these Licchavis if you would like to know what the gods look like there."

When the Licchavis had alighted from their carriages, they approached the Buddha and prostrated. He instructed them in the Dharma, and they were so delighted with his words that they tried in spite of everything to invite him for the following day's meal. The Buddha declined, explaining that he had already been invited by the courtesan Amrapali. Those Licchavi nobles, who, though dignified, were also very playful, snapped their fingers in mock anger and said, "Oh, that mango girl has outdone us again!" Then they respectfully took their leave of the Buddha and departed.

The following day Amrapali had an excellent meal prepared for the community at the mango-grove park, and when it was over, she made a gift of the park "to the Sangha headed by the Buddha."

After the Blessed One had stayed at Amrapali's park as long as he liked, he said to Ananda, "Let us go on to the village of Venugramaka." So everything was made ready, and the Blessed One set off for Venugramaka with a very large company of bhikshus. After he had been living there for a time, he told the great body of monks who were accompanying him to return to Vaishali for the rainy season retreat. He himself would spend the rainy season at Venugramaka. So the bhikshus left, and the Blessed One settled in for the retreat. During the rains, he contracted a serious illness that was accompanied by very severe pain. He bore the pain with equanimity, but still the illness was a dire one that threatened his very life. Thinking that he had not yet taken leave of his close attendants and of the community as a whole, he made a strong effort of will and succeeded in suppressing the illness.

When the illness had passed, Ananda told the Blessed One, "I am so used to seeing you well and at ease that I became very confused and afraid when you were ill. I was only able to console myself because I knew you would not leave us without giving us some instructions for the guidance of the Sangha."

"But Ananda, I have spent forty-five years giving instructions for the guidance of the Sangha. I am not one of those who jealously keep their important teachings in a closed fist. The Dharma has been fully revealed. What more can you expect of me now? Should I declare what direction the Sangha should take? Someone who would do that would be someone who thinks, 'The Sangha is dependent on me.' But a tathagata does not think that way. How could the Sangha depend on me? I am old and decrepit like a broken-down old cart that has to be held together with thongs. I only experience ease in my body by withdrawing my attention from outward sensations and letting it rest in the heart. So the Sangha cannot depend on me.

"Rather than depending on another, taking refuge in another, each of you should be an island. Let your refuge be the Dharma. And how does one make the Dharma his refuge? By practicing the four foundations of mindfulness, that is the way. Now or after I am gone, whoever makes himself an island or the Dharma his island will be the foremost among the Sangha."

Then the Blessed One traveled north by stages until he arrived at the Jetavana outside Shravasti. While he was there, Chunda, Shariputra's personal attendant, arrived carrying his master's robes and bowl. He had carried them the long way north from Nalanda in the Magadhan country where Shariputra had been born and had now passed away in his mother's house after a painful illness.

"We should show these to the Blessed One," said Ananda. So the two monks took Shariputra's robes and bowl in to the Blessed One. Placing their palms together, they bowed to him. Then they said, "The venerable Shariputra has attained the final nirvana. These are his robes and bowl."

The Blessed One remained silent.

"My lord, when Chunda showed me his things and told me he was dead, I felt very confused and afraid. I could hardly see or move."

"Why is that?" the Blessed One replied. "By dying, did he take away from the Sangha the understanding of discipline, meditation, and knowledge that sees things as they are? Did he take with him liberation and understanding?"

"No, lord. The Blessed One is right. But I only thought of how tirelessly he encouraged us and instructed us and helped us progress in the Dharma, how he nurtured and enriched us with his teaching."

"You know well, Ananda," said the Buddha, "that from everything dear and beloved there must be separation. How is it possible that anything composite should not decompose or anything that is born should not die? Venerable Shariputra's passing is like the falling of a main branch from a great and strong, firm and solid tree. The tree continues to grow. So let each of you make himself an island and have no other refuge. Let each of you make the Dharma his island and take no other refuge."

Not long after that, word came that Maudgalyayana had also died. The great disciple had been beaten to death at the instigation of members of one of the other mendicant orders, who deemed he was too great a force for alms and donations coming to the Buddha's Sangha and not to any of the others. When bhikshus asked the Buddha how a person of Maudgalyayana's powers could have been beaten to death, he explained that in a previous life he had temporarily intended to kill his parents. The karmic result of this was that his powers failed when he was attacked.

Once after this, the Buddha was teaching the assembly of monks and he said, "Now when I look out on the assembly it seems empty to me. There is nowhere in the assembly where I can think, 'There Shariputra and Maudgalyayana are to be found.' The tathagatas of the past each had two such accomplished disciples, and so will those of the future. It is wonderful how such disciples give voice to, manifest, and carry out the Tathagata's doctrine and intent. It is wonderful of the Tathagata how, when they are gone, he does not grieve or sorrow for them. For how is it possible that anything that is born should not die?"

ONE DAY, after the Blessed One had finished his alms round and his meal, he called Ananda to come with him, and they went into Vaishali to the Chapala shrine, one of the many beautiful shrines set in lovely parks that adorned that splendid city. When they arrived, Ananda arranged a seat for the Buddha and himself took a seat off to one side. "It is delightful here," said the Blessed One. "Vaishali is a place of many beauties," he went on, and he named its shrines and other beautiful features. "You know, Ananda, if a tathagata wished, he would have the power to live until the end of the age, until the time when the whole world system is destroyed. He could live out what remains of the age."

Not knowing exactly what to make of this, Ananda nodded agreeably. After a few moments, the Buddha repeated the same speech almost identically. Perhaps Ananda was thinking that this was just the kind of thing that old men say to each other on a lovely quiet afternoon. In any case, he only nodded his agreement again. Even after the Buddha had repeated his words for the third time, Ananda could not think of anything to say. So he said nothing. Some minutes passed, and the Tathagata spoke again to tell Ananda that if he wished, he could go about his business. So Ananda took his leave and went to sit under a tree not too far away.

Then Mara came to the Blessed One and stood at a respectful distance off to one side. "It is time now for the Blessed One to attain final nirvana. Now is the time. Now you should attain final nirvana. This would be the right time for the Blessed One's final nirvana. Once you said that you would not attain nirvana finally until all your followers, monastic and lay, men and women, had been well established in the Dharma, both in the doctrine and the practice; until they were capable of realizing the stages of realization on their own and transmitting it to others who then also were capable of attaining realization; until the holy life you taught was widespread and prospering. Now that time has come. It has come to pass. Now is the time for you to pass on, die. You can enter nirvana now utterly. Now is the time for you to do it. Now."

"Peace, Mara," said the Buddha. "You may rejoice. The Tathagata will die soon. In three months, the Blessed One will enter the unborn, the deathless—nirvana—finally and completely. The Buddha's parinirvana will be in three months."

Then the Blessed One loosed his hold on the connection with the formations making up his earthly life, which he had been holding in the grip of his will since Venugramaka. At that moment the earth shook with a deep and fearsome rumbling that sent a shiver through the whole of existence.

When the rumbling in the earth had passed, Ananda, who was rather alarmed, came to his master's side. He bowed with his palms together and sat down and respectfully began questioning him about the great tremor. The Blessed One explained to him the relationship between the elements that brings earthquakes about, and then enumerated some of the kinds of occasions on which they are produced. One of the occasions he enumerated was the relinquishment of his life force by a buddha. And this, he said, was the reason the earth had shaken just now. Then the Blessed One recounted to Ananda all that had taken place between Mara and himself since he had quit Kapilavastu and the householder's life.

When the significance of all this dawned on Ananda, he immediately prostrated to the Buddha and beseeched him to remain. "Lord, please live out the age out of compassion for all beings," he begged. A second and a third time Ananda now made his request. Finally the Buddha explained to him that the time for such requesting was now past. And he sadly related the many occasions over the past twenty-five years when, as earlier that afternoon, he had dropped broad hints that might have prompted Ananda to request him to live out the age. Now he had irrevocably relinquished his hold on his life and would die and enter nirvana utterly and completely in three months.

Then he reminded Ananda again that separation from what is dear and beloved is inevitable, for everything that is compounded is subject to dissolution and everything that arises ceases.

Later that day, at the Kutagara Hall outside the city, he told the assembly of the bhikshus that were with him that he would soon attain the final nirvana, parinirvana. He encouraged them to exert themselves in the Dharma and the discipline he had taught them, to be diligent in their mindfulness and thus attain perfection.

The following morning the Blessed One went into Vaishali to gather alms. As he was climbing a hill on the way back, he paused and turned his whole upper body, head and shoulders together, in the gesture that is known as the elephant's gaze and looked back upon that radiant city with the sunlight glittering upon its gold-, silver-, and copper-roofed towers. "This will be the Tathagata's last look at Vaishali," he told Ananda.

"Yes, lord," the old attendant replied.

"So let us travel on now to Bhanda village."

"Yes, lord," came the answer.

IN THE TIME that remained to him, the Blessed One traveled northwest by slow stages, stopping sometimes for a period of weeks in one place to rest and give detailed teachings to the large company of bhikshus traveling with him. The way led through Vrijian and then Mallan country along the Hiranyavati River, roughly in the direction of Kapilavastu.

After staying a fairly long time at Bhoganagara, he proceeded to the region of Pava and stopped in the mango grove of a goldsmith named Chunda. When Chunda heard that he was so fortunate as to have the Buddha staying in his mango grove, he rushed out to greet him, prostrated and sat down off to one side. Then the Blessed One gave instruction in the Dharma to all who were present, following which Chunda invited the Buddha and the Sangha to his house for the following day's meal. The Blessed One accepted by remaining silent.

Chunda had quantities of good food prepared by the next day, including particularly large amounts of a special pork dish. When the Buddha arrived at his house and had taken his seat, he told Chunda, "Serve the pork dish to me alone and serve the other food to the community." Chunda complied. Then a little later the Blessed One added, "Take the rest of that pork dish and bury it in a hole somewhere, for I see no one else in the whole universe with its gods, men, and other beings other than the Tathagata who would be able to digest it." Then, when the meal was over, the Buddha instructed everyone present in the Dharma and departed.

Within a few hours the Buddha suffered a violent attack of gastric illness with dire pain and severe bleeding of the bowel. He bore the pain with equanimity, mindful and aware. After a time, he said to Ananda, "Come, let us go on to Kushinagara."

On the way to Kushinagara, the Blessed One left the road and told Ananda to prepare a seat for him at the foot of a tree, saying he was tired and needed to sit down. Then he asked Ananda to bring him some water to drink from the nearby stream.

"Lord, a whole long line of carts has just gone through that stream. It is all churned up, and the water is full of mud. Wait just a while and we'll come to the Hiranyavati where you can drink pure water and cool your limbs."

"I am thirsty, Ananda, and would drink. Please get me some water," the Buddha said again. Ananda was still reluctant, and only when the Blessed One had asked him for the third time did he accede to his wish and go to the stream for water. When he came to dip his bowl, the stream, which was thick and brown with churned-up dirt, suddenly turned sparkling clear in that place. Amazed, he returned to the Buddha. He knelt and gave him the water, saying, "Let the Blessed One drink! Let the Blessed One drink!"

In a short while a Mallan named Kusala came along the road, a man who was a follower of the teaching of Arada Kalama. He saw the Blessed One sitting at the foot of the tree, approached and greeted him, then prostrated and sat down off to one side. He began telling the Blessed One about the prodigious meditative feats of his master, Arada. The Tathagata listened for a while and then began recounting to Kusala some of his own meditation experiences, which seemed to surpass those of Arada. In the end Kusala was overcome with awe. He said that in speaking with the Blessed One his attachment to his master had blown away like a dry leaf. He begged to become the Buddha's follower. The Blessed One accepted him and gave him the triple refuge.

Kusala then sent a man to fetch two robes of cloth woven from threads of pure gold. He requested the Blessed One to accept these, and the Buddha responded that he would accept one and Ananda could take the other. Kusala presented the Blessed One and Ananda with the shining robes. Then he expressed his gratitude, prostrated, and went his way.

When he had gone, Ananda dressed the Blessed One in both the robes. As soon as they were on his body, their brilliance seemed to fade away. Ananda said, "It is truly amazing how brilliant and lustrous the Blessed One's body has become. It has made the brightness of the golden robes seem to disappear like nothing!"

"There are two occasions, Ananda," said the Buddha, "when a tathagata's skin acquires this extraordinary brilliant glow — on the eve of his enlightenment and on the eve of his final nirvana. And in fact, Ananda, in the last watch of this coming night, between the twin shala trees in the shala grove in the turn of the river before Kushinagara, the Tathagata will attain his final nirvana."

Then the Blessed One got up from his seat and continued on his way till he came to the river. There he bathed and drank. Then he crossed the river and lay down on his right side to rest in a mango grove on its far bank.

As he was lying there, he said to Ananda, "As for Chunda the goldsmith, it is possible he might be afflicted with remorse when he hears how the Blessed One fared after receiving his last meal from him. You should tell Chunda the smith that the last food given to a tathagata before his enlightenment and the last given before his final nirvana bring particular merit to the giver. He has acquired great merit, and great good fortune will be his in the future. Tell him that I said this; it should counter his remorse."

Then the Blessed One rose and walked till he came to the shala grove. There he told Ananda to prepare him a bed between the twin trees. Those trees were covered with blossoms out of season, and the grove was thronged with gods who had come to be present at the

Blessed One's final nirvana, his parinirvana. For a great distance all around, there was not a space the size of a hair tip not occupied by deities.

Realizing that the Blessed One would soon be gone, Ananda began to ask him all manner of questions, trying to sew up loose ends before it was too late.

"How should we treat the Tathagata's remains?" he asked.

"Do not make a big point of venerating the Tathagata's remains. Strive for your own attainment. Diligent but controlled, devote yourself to your own good. Let the brahmins and householders concern themselves with the Blessed One's remains."

Ananda questioned him further, and the Blessed One spoke about the various circumstances in which it was proper to build stupas, monuments, to house a tathagata's relics and to remind people of the Tathagata.

This talk of monuments to commemorate the Tathagata seemed to be too much for Ananda. He excused himself and went into a nearby shed, where he leaned against the inside of the door and wept. "My teacher who is so compassionate and kind to me is about to attain the ultimate nirvana, and I am still so passion-ridden and have not attained realization!" This is what he thought to himself as the tears poured from his eyes.

The Blessed One was being attended by some other bhikshus. "Where is Ananda?" he asked them.

"He is in that shed, crying," he was told.

"Go to Ananda and tell him, 'Your teacher calls you,'" the Blessed One told one of the bhikshus. The monk brought Ananda this message. Then Ananda returned to the Blessed One and bowed to him with his palms together and stood off to one side. "Ananda," said the Buddha, "have I not often told you we must be separated from what we hold dear? How is it possible that what is born should not die? As for you, you have served me well and with great kindness for many years, served me with your body, with your speech, and with your mind. You have laid up much merit, Ananda. Just be diligent for a little while, and you will attain the goal.

"Now, bhikshus, you should know that all the tathagatas of the past have had an attendant like Ananda, and the future ones will as well. Ananda is full of wisdom about how to serve a tathagata. Ananda has these wonderful qualities, monks: When he arrives somewhere, the community is glad to see him. When he speaks, they are delighted by what they hear. When he is silent again, they feel they would still like to hear more."

Picking at straws, Ananda said to the Tathagata, "Please let the Blessed One not attain final nirvana here in this remote place. There are great cities in the world full of illustrious followers of yours who could surround the Tathagata and honor him at the time of his final nirvana. It does not seem suitable for you to part from us here." Then the Blessed One told Ananda how in a past age a great city, an imperial capital ruled over by a great king, had stood on that spot.

"Now, Ananda," he said, "go in to Kushinagara and tell the Mallans that the Blessed One's parinirvana will take place tonight in the last watch."

Ananda went into Kushinagara and informed the Mallans of the event about to take place in their shala grove. When they heard the news, the Mallans were stunned, then torn with grief. For more than fifty years the Buddha had roamed the country, shedding illumination all about him. It seemed impossible for this support to fall away. As they grasped the reality of the Blessed One's passing, the Mallans began to tear their hair and lament. "The Blessed One is leaving us!" they cried. "The eye of the world will be gone!"

Soon those aggrieved and mournful Mallans, children and old people and all, were gathering at the shala grove to bid farewell to the Blessed One. There were so many of them that it would have taken until dawn for all to file past and pay their last respects to the Tathagata. So Ananda had each clan provide a representative. Then all those representatives were presented one by one to the Blessed One, whose breaths were already numbered, and he acknowledged the homage of each of them.

At that time there was a wandering ascetic staying in Kushinagara, whose name was Subhadra. He was an earnest seeker, but his doubts about what path to follow were unresolved. He thought to himself, "Here a tathagata is passing away. He is still here, but in one or two hours, there will no longer be a buddha in the world. I know that if I can talk to him, he can resolve my doubts."

So Subhadra made his way through the crowds of people to where the Buddha lay, surrounded by his close attendants and other monks. He approached Ananda and requested to be permitted to exchange a few words with the Blessed One.

"Please don't think of disturbing the Blessed One at such a time, Subhadra. The Blessed One is tired."

The young man sensed his precious opportunity slipping away and pressed his request a second and a third time. As Ananda was finally about to send him away, the Buddha spoke.

"Ananda, do not keep Subhadra away. Let him see the Tathagata. What he will ask will not trouble me, because he genuinely thirsts for understanding."

So the young ascetic was permitted to see the Blessed One in his last hour. He approached him and exchanged greetings and other words of courtesy. When the amenities were complete, he prostrated to the Blessed One and sat down off to one side.

"Master Gautama," said the young man, "there are these six great teachers, heads of great mendicant orders with many followers. They all teach different doctrines. Is it possible that all of them have had direct knowledge and realization as they claim?"

"Subhadra," the Buddha replied, "drop for now this question of whether or not this or that teacher has direct realization. Hear me attentively now, for I will teach you the Dharma."

"Yes, lord."

"In whatever teaching of doctrine and practice the Noble Eightfold Path is not found, among the followers are not found the first monk, the second monk, the third monk, or the fourth monk, that is, those who attain the first, the second, the third, or the fourth stages of realization. But in whatever doctrine and practice the Eightfold Path is present, there you will also find the first monk, the second monk, the third monk, and the fourth. Subhadra, it is only in this doctrine and practice that the first, second, third, and fourth monks are found. The assemblies of other doctrines are empty of monks who realize the four stages.

"Subhadra, I went forth into homelessness seeking victory at the age of twenty-nine. Since then, more than fifty years have passed. I tell you, Subhadra, outside this Dharma, there are no monks who tread even a part of the true path. But if monks follow the path I have set forth properly, the world will not lack for arhats."

"It is wonderful, lord," responded Subhadra. "It is surely as you say. Please, lord, receive me. I take refuge in the Buddha, I take refuge in the Dharma, I take refuge in the Sangha. Please may the Blessed One accept me into the order of bhikshus."

The Blessed One gave his permission for this to be done. So Subhadra became the last to be received into the order by the Buddha. Not long after his admission, he went into solitary retreat, where he practiced meditation intensively, earnest but controlled. Soon he attained direct and independent knowledge of the Dharma. He attained the realization of an arhat in which, through the absence of clinging, all his defilements were purified.

When Subhadra had taken his leave and gone, the Blessed One said to Ananda, "When the Blessed One is gone, you might think that the teacher is gone, that you no longer have a teacher. This is not true. The Dharma, the discipline, and the practice that I taught you will be your teacher after I am gone."

Then he addressed all the bhikshus who were nearby and said, "There might be some among you who have a doubt or a problem concerning the Buddha, the Dharma, or the Sangha. If that is so, ask about it now, so you will not later say to yourselves regretfully, 'I was face to face with the teacher, and I did not ask.' "

The monks, who had now gathered from throughout the grove, stood encircling the recumbent Buddha. There was silence.

"Perhaps you do not ask out of respect for the teacher or because of embarrassment. If that is so, tell your question to a friend so that he can ask it."

Again there was silence. Finally Ananda spoke up.

"Lord, it is amazing, it is wonderful. I feel confident that there is not one monk here who has any doubts concerning the teacher, the Dharma, the Sangha, the path, or the manner of progressing along the path."

"You speak your words out of confidence, Ananda, but the Tathagata knows with direct knowledge that there is not one bhikshu in all these five hundred who has a doubt concerning the Buddha, the Dharma, the Sangha, the path, or the way of progressing upon it. The least advanced of them has entered the stream, has attained the first stage of realization, is no longer subject to falling away, has achieved certainty, and is destined for enlightenment.

"Truly, monks, I declare this to you. It is in the nature of whatever is formed to dissolve. Attain perfection through diligence."

The Buddha stopped speaking. He entered successively the first, the second, the third, and then the fourth level of meditative absorption. Then he entered the formless realm and progressed through the levels of meditation based on boundless space, boundless consciousness, nothingness, and "neither perception nor nonperception." Then he passed to the cessation of perception and feeling.

Then Ananda said to Aniruddha, who was standing by, "The Blessed One has attained parinirvana."

"No, Ananda," said the other, "not yet. Only the cessation of perception and feeling."

Then the Blessed One passed back down through the levels again until he reached the first level of meditation. Then again he ascended from the first, to the second, to the third, and then to fourth level. Then he attained the utter extinction of final nirvana, parinirvana.

There was a profound rumbling within the earth and a vast thundering in the heavens.

Notes

In passages quoted from material using Pali terms, Sanskrit equivalents have been substituted for the sake of reader continuity.

1. *Anguttara-nikaya*, III, 38; quoted in Bhikku Nyanamoli, *Life of the Buddha* (Kandy, Ceylon: Buddhist Publication Society, 1972), pp. 8–9; wording slightly adapted.
2. Ibid., p. 9.
3. *Majjhima-nikaya* 26; in Nyanamoli, p. 10.
4. *Majjhima-nikaya* 36, 100; in Nyanamoli, p. 10.
5. *Majjhima-nikaya* 100; in Nyanamoli, p. 14.
6. *Majjhima-nikaya* 36, 85, 100; in Nyanamoli, pp. 17–21.
7. *Majjhima-nikaya* 26; in Nyanamoli, p. 29.
8. Nyanamoli, p. 30.
9. Ibid., p. 42.
10. Ibid., pp. 42–43.
11. Ibid., p. 52, with slight variations.
12. *Samyutta-nikaya* IV, 24–25; in Nyanamoli, p. 64.
13. Ashvajit's formulation was enshrined by tradition and is still often used as a mantra. In Sanskrit it is (*Om*) *ye dharma hetu-prabhava hetum tesham tathagatah hyavadat tesham cha yo nirodha evam vadi mahashramanah* (*svaha*).
14. *Majjhima-nikaya* 128; in Nyanamoli, p. 113.
15. *Mahavagga* 10; in Nyanamoli, p. 116.
16. *Majjhima-nikaya* 62; in Nyanamoli, p. 123.
17. *Sutta-vibhanga*, para. 1; in Nyanamoli, p. 128; wording slightly adapted.
18. *Cullavagga* 7, in Nyanamoli, p. 271; verse slightly adapted.
19. *Digha-nikaya* 16; in Nyanamoli, p. 296.

Shambhala Dragon Editions

(Continued on next page)

The Myth of Freedom and the Way of Meditation, by Chögyam Trungpa.

Nine-Headed Dragon River, by Peter Matthiessen.

Returning to Silence: Zen Practice in Daily Life, by Dainin Katagiri. Foreword by Robert Thurman.

Seeking the Heart of Wisdom: The Path of Insight Meditation, by Joseph Goldstein & Jack Kornfield. Foreword by H. H. the Dalai Lama.

Shambhala: The Sacred Path of the Warrior, by Chögyam Trungpa.

The Shambhala Dictionary of Buddhism and Zen.

The Spiritual Teaching of Ramana Maharshi, by Ramana Maharshi. Foreword by C. G. Jung.

Tao Teh Ching, by Lao Tzu. Translated by John C. H. Wu.

The Tibetan Book of the Dead: The Great Liberation through Hearing in the Bardo. Translated with commentary by Francesca Fremantle & Chögyam Trungpa.

Vitality, Energy, Spirit: A Taoist Sourcebook. Translated & edited by Thomas Cleary.

Wen-tzu: Understanding the Mysteries, by Lao-tzu. Translated by Thomas Cleary.

Worldly Wisdom: Confucian Teachings of the Ming Dynasty. Translated & edited by J. C. Cleary.

Zen Essence: The Science of Freedom. Translated & edited by Thomas Cleary.

The Zen Teachings of Master Lin-chi. Translated by Burton Watson.